On the Plains
with Custer and Hancock

whose mind was made up. Not intending any harm to
them, we did pause to consider their just grounds of fear,
& moved on, camping till afternoon within a few hundred yards of their village, after a march of ten miles, and
doing nothing more than from that distance.

The Indian village was situated in a beautiful grove on the
north fork of Pawnee, a most charming spot; the buffalo grass,
which was just beginning to grow, was soft as velvet to the feet.
Here this lonely abode the red men had been living, remote
from the public highway, in peace & quietness. But now
the army, like a distracted earthquake, had come to demolish
their habitations, and send them fleeing, homeless, for their lives.
Guards were stationed around our camp to prevent the soldiers
from going to the village. A few poor Indians found grazing
near us were sent to the Indians. Soon after our encampment, General Hancock summoned the principal Chiefs, and
Roman Nose, Medicine Wolf, Bull Bear, and Grey Beard, chief
names, were not long in answering the summons. They informed the General that the women & children were so terrified
on seeing the troops approach, and fearing that they would be
all massacred, as the Indians were at Sand Creek, ran
off, leaving everything behind them; and that the Squaws,
too, who there mostly dismounted, had fled with them.
In the course of the talk, Roman Nose showed his bold and
fearless spirit. When General Hancock inquired, some
what decidedly, why the women & children had fled on his
approach; the Indian asked him whether the women and
children of the whites were not more timid than the men
not men; being warriors one not afraid of any thing; that
he & his comrades were men & warriors, and were not
afraid of General Hancock and his troops, but that the women
and children were afraid, and had run away. Roman
Nose also asked the General if he had not heard of the
butchery of Indians at Sand Creek, by U.S. troops

On the Plains
with Custer and Hancock

THE JOURNAL OF
ISAAC COATES, ARMY SURGEON

W.J.D. KENNEDY

Foreword by Jerome A. Greene

Johnson Books
BOULDER

Published in the United States by Johnson Books, a division of Johnson Publishing Company, 1880 South 57th Court, Boulder, Colorado 80301.

9   8   7   6   5   4   3   2   1

Cover design by Debra B. Topping
Cover photos by Kansas State Historical Society and private collection

Library of Congress Cataloging-in-Publication Data
Coates, Isaac Taylor, 1834–1883.
  On the plains with Custer and Hancock: the journal of Isaac Coates, Army surgeon / [edited by] W.J.D. Kennedy
      p.   cm.
  Includes bibliographical references (p.   ) and index.
  ISBN 1-55566-183-1 (cloth: alk. paper).—ISBN 1-55566-184-X
  (paperback: alk. paper)
  1. Indians of North America—Wars—1866–1895—Personal narratives.
2. Coates, Isaac Taylor, 1834–1883.   3. United States. Army.
Cavalry, 7th—Biography.   4. Physicians—United States—Biography.
5. Custer, George Armstrong, 1839–1876.   6. Hancock, Winfield Scott,
1824–1886.   I. Kennedy, W. J. D., 1924– .   II. Title.
E83.866.C63   1996
973.8′1′092—dc20   96-32360
[B]   CIP

Printed in the United States by
Johnson Printing
1880 South 57th Court
Boulder, Colorado 80301

 Printed on recycled paper with soy ink

Contents

For my dear wife Lucretia—
Isaac Coates would be proud
of his progeny

Foreword

IN THE SPRING AND SUMMER of 1867, the plains of Kansas became a backdrop for the converging consequences of two of the most emotionally charged events in the history of Indian-white relations in the United States. Less than three years earlier, on November 24, 1864, Colorado territorial militia had wantonly destroyed a Cheyenne village at Sand Creek, Colorado Territory, killing men, women, and children in a particularly brutal attack. Sand Creek proved a wrenchingly controversial affair, applauded by some people and condemned by others. Conversely, in a more recent incident, on December 21, 1866, Teton Sioux warriors had overwhelmed an army detachment near Fort Phil Kearny, Wyoming Territory, wiping out eighty soldiers in an incident that also seared the national consciousness and promoted public outcry. The two events symbolized the wildly discordant state of affairs between whites and Indians in the trans-Mississippi West and, especially, represented real trauma for the Cheyennes, whose comparatively small society had to absorb the physical and psychological shock of the human and material losses at Sand Creek.

The events brought profound repercussions among their respective peoples, which were manifest in early 1867. Sand Creek promoted a simmering sense of distrust and enmity within the councils of the Cheyennes and their affiliated tribes, such as the Sioux and Arapahos. The Fort Phil Kearny "massacre" provoked a government response that demanded strong military intimidation of the western tribes to forestall future incidents of kind. Amid these circumstances was born the impetus for a military campaign against the tribes of Kansas in the spring of 1867 led by Major General Winfield S. Hancock. The operation was less important for its immediate results than for its unsettling long-range impact on U.S.

government–Indian relations throughout the Great Plains. Of somewhat less significance at the time, but of great interest today, was the fact that Hancock's movement constituted the inaugural chapter in the Indian-fighting career of Lieutenant Colonel George Armstrong Custer, the army's *beau sabreur* of the Civil War, who would one day lead his regiment to defeat at the hands of Sioux and Cheyenne Indians along Montana's Little Bighorn River.

In its contribution to knowledge of the Hancock-Custer campaign, the journal of Dr. Isaac T. Coates, as edited herein by W.J.D. Kennedy, is of inestimable value. Coates, a Pennsylvanian with Civil War service with the navy and postwar service with his home state's volunteers in Texas, had an adventuresome spirit that led him to seek appointment as an act-ing assistant surgeon with the army for duty in the West. Fortuitously, his application coincided with the upcoming Hancock expedition to intimi-date the Indians. Even more fortunate was Coates's decision to record (possibly initially in a diary) some of the events he participated in and wit-nessed during his sojourn on the plains in 1867 and to later prepare the journal presented in this volume. Among Coates's most significant con-tributions are the descriptions of his introduction to army life on the plains; a rendering of Hancock's council with the Cheyennes at Fort Larned, Kansas, in April 1867; a wonderfully vivid account of the inci-dent at the Cheyenne village on Pawnee Fork; a verbal portrait of Chief Roman Nose; a description of Custer's pursuit of the Indians; and a grip-ping account of the perils and joys of buffalo hunting on the Kansas plains. Editor Kennedy's well-written and insightful commentary com-pares Coates's remarks with those of other period sources, further illumi-nating the events of Hancock's campaign. Where Coates's recollections lapse, following Hancock's personal withdrawal from the field, Kennedy ably completes the story of the expedition with a narrative of Custer's sub-sequent campaigning. Fraught with turmoil and controversy, these cam-paigns resulted in Custer's court-martial and subsequent suspension from the service. Coates's testimony at Custer's trial is presented in its entirety.

As Kennedy relates, the Coates narrative turned up years ago in an attic in Minneapolis. A valuable record, it adds a new dimension to our knowledge about what happened on the plains of Kansas one hundred thirty years ago. As such, it constitutes another important contribution to the broad mosaic that is the history of the American West.

Jerome A. Greene

Preface

ONE DAY, WHEN my wife, Lucretia, was visiting her home in Minneapolis, her mother asked if she would like to see some notes written by her great-grandfather. Upstairs in the attic, lying on the floor among piles of old magazines and books, was a small bundle of hand-written pages wrapped loosely in worn, brown paper. On the outside, in faint pencil, was written, "Account of Indian Campaign with Hancock and Custer in 1867 by Dr. I. T. Coates."

All we knew about him, at first, was that his name was Isaac Coates and that he was Lucretia's great-grandfather, nothing more. The family had given no more thought to him than most families give to great-grandfathers, but through a hundred years of packing and moving and unpacking, his journal, as the bundle turned out to be, had been preserved intact by each person to whom it had been entrusted. Yet no one had read the notes for many years, and no one living knew what they contained. Not only did they change hands many times, but they may also have traveled repeatedly back and forth across the country.

Isaac Coates's journal may have journeyed with him from Chester, Pennsylvania, to Reno, Nevada, to Pueblo, Colorado, and to Socorro, New Mexico, and wherever else he practiced medicine in the western United States. If Isaac did take his notes to Socorro, then after his death his thirteen-year-old son, Harold, might have brought them back to Chester where Harold was to live with his Uncle Charles Morton and his Aunt Annie, Isaac's sister.

More likely, perhaps, Isaac gave the notes to Annie Morton for safekeeping sometime in the early 1870s, before his trips to South America and the western United States. Annie would, in turn, have given them to the adult Harold when he married and moved away. Harold and his wife, Florence (Lucretia's grandfather and grandmother), lived at various times in Salt Lake City, St. Louis, and Philadelphia. After Harold's death in 1931, Florence moved from Philadelphia to Minneapolis. Sometime afterward, probably in the 1940s, Florence gave Isaac's notes to her daughter (Lucretia's mother), who stored them in her attic until giving them to Lucretia. In what may have been its last journey, the journal then traveled with us from Minneapolis to Boulder, Colorado.

Now that we had the journal, the question was what to do with it. We were anxious to find out what was inside, of course, but because of its seemingly fragile condition we were afraid of damaging it. The rare-manuscript experts we consulted advised us to handle the journal as little as possible and then only while wearing clean cotton gloves. We decided the best way to record what we found, assuming that we would be able to read it, was to dictate the contents into a tape recorder. The system worked quite well. We read the journal a second time to check words and spelling, and this time was easier—because our hands were not trembling so much.

Except for an esoteric reference here and there, the pages were entirely legible and understandable. As we read Isaac's story, written in his flowing script, we began to wonder what sort of man he was, what happened to him after his service with the cavalry, where he lived, where he died. We read his account of his trip on the immigrant train, his meeting with General Custer, the bitter cold of his first night on the plains, moonlight marches, buffalo hunts, and his observations about the army and General Hancock. We were struck by his sympathy and admiration for the Indian warriors whom he watched struggle against what he foresaw was the inevitable destruction of their culture. Remarkably, he continued to hold that respect even after examining the mutilated bodies of fellow soldiers killed by the same Indians. We thought he must have been a kind and generous man, with a quick wit and an ability to laugh at himself. He certainly was physically tough and quite brave.

We soon became fascinated with this person emerging from the shadows of 125 years. Gradually we felt more and more responsible for uncov-

ering the details of his life and putting them in some coherent and permanent form. To begin with we wanted to find out whether somewhere,
in the house in Minneapolis or perhaps even in some obscure book or
journal, there might be some passing mention of Isaac Coates. The Boulder Public Library and the books on the much-written-about General
Custer seemed a good place to start. The first one we chose was *The
Court-Martial of General George Armstrong Custer* by Dr. Lawrence R.
Frost, which, to our amazement, had eleven references to Isaac Coates.
Someone else knew he existed! We were on our way.

By coincidence, at about the same time we were beginning our search
for other clues about Isaac Coates, Lucretia's mother moved out of her
home in Minneapolis and into an apartment. As we tidied up the place
for the real estate people, we excitedly discovered, back in the dark corners
of closets and under the eaves of the attic, metal cans and cardboard boxes
filled with family papers, photographs, and objects dating back to the
early nineteenth century. Here was a photograph of Isaac Coates, in a
navy lieutenant's uniform, taken before he left that service in 1865. For
the first time, we knew what he looked like. There was also a friendly card
from an officer in the Peruvian navy dated May 1872 and a photograph of
a handsome Brazilian lady, with an affectionate note written on the back.
Among other papers, we found a few pages of a narrative written by Isaac
for his son about their trip together down the Madeira River in Brazil.

Also at about this time, we received a letter from Randy Johnson, co-
author with Nancy Allan of *Find Custer! The Kidder Tragedy*. Randy had
found Lucretia's name through the University of Pennsylvania. He was
doing research for a paper on, of all people, Dr. Isaac Coates. He suggested that we write to the National Archives, and he even filled out the
necessary forms for us to sign. We soon received records of Isaac's military
service and copies of correspondence between Isaac and the surgeon general's office. Later, the people at the National Archives helped us obtain
microfilm copies of the proceedings of the Custer court-martial, all of it in
longhand. Gail Pietrzyk, of the University of Pennsylvania Archives and
Records Center, produced valuable material from her files and also

recommended additional places for us to look. Douglas McManis, of the American Geographical Society, found copies of letters Isaac Coates had written to the society in 1879 and 1880. Linda Rossi, of the Academy of Natural Sciences of Philadelphia, gave us more information and sound advice. With the help of a growing circle of new friends, whose only connection with us was a shared enthusiasm for finding out more about this man, we were gathering correspondence from and records about the last sixteen years of Isaac Coates's life.

In the boxes of papers we had carried away from the house in Minneapolis, we found a long letter to Lucretia's mother from her Uncle Howard Morton, Isaac's nephew, who knew Isaac well. The letter, written in 1939, told us more about Isaac Coates personally than had any other source. The only other reference to his personality that we found was Custer's affectionate remarks about him in *My Life on the Plains*. Howard had written: "Your grandfather was an idealist and a natural-born wanderer. He was a great admirer of the female sex and a gallant. He was a man of wonderful charm and most polished address. He ran the whole gamut of classical writers—his reading was simply prodigious. The Latin and Greek writings and writers of the world were his daily pabulum. He was a truly remarkable man, and I feel that I, personally, owe to him my love for literature. He spoke Spanish with great fluency. As a young man he travelled much in Europe, and took on one of these [trips] his young brother, Aquilla. He never could make money or save it."

By this time we had become thoroughly captivated by Isaac Coates. We decided to follow in his footsteps, hoping that there might be some remnant of the landscape he had seen so long ago on the march across Kansas. We drove to Fort Larned, now splendidly restored by the National Park Service, where park service historian George Elmore was generous with his time and advice. He had explored the route of the Seventh Cavalry and knew exactly where the events described in Isaac Coates's journal had taken place. Armed with copies of Lieutenant Jackson's 1867 maps of the route of the march, we drove west of Fort Larned and parked our car by the Pawnee Fork, near the site where Isaac Coates had camped on Saturday night, April 13, 1867. We walked to the top of a small hill and looked out over the plains beyond, where Isaac Coates and General Hancock's soldiers had seen three hundred mounted Indian warriors in a line, "not still for a moment. Every horse was in motion." We stood there for a long time, watching the empty prairie and the grass waving in the wind.

Following a rough dirt road along the Pawnee Fork, we found the site of the Indian village. Although no longer "a most charming spot" or "a beautiful grove," as Isaac Coates had described it, the river valley is still wooded in places, now an island in a sea of wheat. We pushed our way through a tangle of brush and standing and fallen trees, looking for, but not really expecting to find, some sign that this had once been the favorite camping place for generations of Cheyenne families. We found no teepee poles or buffalo robes but did see pieces of charred wood. Were they from farmers burning weeds twenty years ago or from fifty-year-old wildfires? Or were they the remains of the fire that consumed the Indian village by order of General Hancock? We imagined the latter.

In some ways Lucretia and I had prepared for our search for Isaac Coates even before we read his journal. We had a long-standing interest in western history and had collected quite a good library of books on the subject. And there was another connection with Sherman, Sheridan, and Custer, but on my side of the family. Early in his journal, Isaac Coates writes about riding the immigrant train from Philadelphia to Chicago and trying to get some sleep after a long day of travel. He notes, with the tolerance that characterizes his attitude about other people throughout the journal, there was "a good deal of hilarity on the wing—and always a chance to learn something, if you will." Which brings me to my forebears. There is a chance, slight but enough to be enjoyable, that the "rich Irish brogue" Isaac heard was being spoken by my grandfather and his brothers, who had just landed in the United States and were bound for St. Paul, Minnesota. Two of the brothers, Martin and my grandfather, Roger, were master gunsmiths. Their gun and outdoor-supply store, Kennedy Bros. Arms Company, was a well-known St. Paul business from 1867 until it closed in 1962. Just how many of the Kennedy brothers came over from the "old country" in 1867 we do not know, but another brother, Jeremiah, probably came along with Martin and Roger. My great-uncle John arrived a few years later with a price on his head for having started a riot in Ireland. He went off to Canada and achieved the distinction of having a second price put on his head for being chief of cavalry in Louis Riel's Red River Rebellion. Riel was eventually tried for treason and hanged, but, as far as we know, John did not meet the same end.

Thirty years after the battle of the Little Bighorn, a St. Paul newspaper described George Armstrong Custer's visit to Kennedy Bros. Arms Company early in 1876. Custer ordered a specially designed hunting knife with a buffalo-horn "sawback" handle and chatted with my grandfather while it was being made. The knife was reported to have been in Custer's belt just before his last battle. My grandfather said later that he could not remember if he had made any charge for the knife. Other army officers who visited the Irish brothers' store were generals Grant, Sherman, Sheridan, and Terry. During the 1880s, two regular customers were ranchers Theodore Roosevelt and the Marquis de Mores, for whom the Kennedys made a number of shotguns and rifles.

We know that Isaac Coates died in Socorro, New Mexico, but not why he died at the relatively young age of forty-nine. Neither Socorro, whose town records were destroyed by fire early in this century, nor the state of New Mexico have any record of Isaac's death. With the help of the Socorro County Historical Society, we searched microfilms of newspapers on file at the public library but were unable to find any papers published near the time of Isaac's death. We did find a small advertisement published in the *Socorro Sunday Sun* of June 10, 1883, offering the medical services of "Doctors Sherman and Coates, Physicians and Surgeons," giving their address as "on Court Street near the Plaza." We walked up Court Street from the lovely, old New Mexican plaza past historic buildings, one of which may have been Isaac Coates's office, where he last practiced medicine and, perhaps, where he died.

Among the many puzzles our research has not solved, and probably never will, is the question of just when Isaac wrote his account of his experiences with the Seventh Cavalry. Some of the entries seem to have been taken directly from his original notes on the march, as he uses the present tense at times and his emotions seem fresh and unrehearsed. However, other entries were clearly written in subsequent years. For example, he compares the disastrous consequences of Hancock's burning of the Indian village with the Chicago fire catastrophe of 1871. In a comment about racial equality in Chicago public schools, he refers to the Fifteenth Amendment of the Constitution, which was ratified by Congress in 1870. Therefore, it was probably some time between 1871 and 1883 that Isaac Coates sat down with his notes and wrote his journal. But we can narrow the time frame if we accept the proposition that he would not have written the journal after July 1876, when news of the battle of the Little Bighorn first reached the East. (We know he was in Pennsylvania because he gave the Chester Centennial Oration on July Fourth.) It is hard to imagine Isaac Coates, who emerges from his narrative as a kind and loyal man, writing blithely about his former comrades in the Seventh Cavalry if he had known that they were lying dead on the Montana plains. Probably, then, he wrote his journal in the early 1870s, perhaps during a visit to Chester between trips to South America.

For us, the greatest mystery about Isaac Coates's journal is why the story stops abruptly with an account of a buffalo hunt in May 1867. He wrote in a letter to the surgeon general dated April 21, 1869, that he was "the only medical officer with the *active* [his emphasis] Seventh Cavalry in the famous Campaign of 1867 under General Custer." Therefore, he must have been the doctor who examined the bodies of Lieutenant Kidder and his party, who were killed by Indians early in July 1867. Later, Isaac Coates was nearly killed himself in a battle with Indians near Fort Wallace. He rode at Custer's right side, a potentially dangerous place to be, he wrote, during the marches across Kansas and into Colorado. Why, with his inquiring mind, keen powers of observation, and sense of drama, did he not record what he saw in those months of hard riding and fighting? We will never know.

We have collected scattered and unconnected bits of information about Isaac's later life, enough to know in general how he spent his last sixteen years. But we prefer to think of him as the young man who had left his home in Chester only four weeks before, riding in the moonlight of a cold April night on the plains, wrapped in his army overcoat with a blanket over his knees and feeling "quite comfortable."

The task of finding Isaac Coates was made immeasurably more pleasant and productive by people we have met only by telephone and letter. Some of them, those who pointed out the trail, were already mentioned. Others who will always have our gratitude include Patricia O'Donnell, of the Friends Historical Library, Swarthmore College; Nancy Sherbert, of the Kansas State Historical Society; Chris Templin and Florence Sankowicz, of the Delaware County Historical Society; Kelly Lynch, of *Harper's New Monthly Magazine*; Katherine Wyatt, of the Nebraska State Historical Society; Kitty Deernose, of the National Park Service; Ann Upton, of the Quaker Collection, Haverford College; Whitney Anderson, of the Catalog of American Portraits, the Smithsonian Institution; Joseph Schwarz, Stuart Butler, Robert Richardson, Gary Morgan, and DeAnne Blanton, of the National Archives; and Paula Fleming and Janet Kennelly, of the National Museum of Natural History, the Smithsonian Institution. To our regret, we did not record names of the many people in the Reference Department of the Boulder Public Library, in the Socorro Public Library, and in the Western History Department of the Denver Public Library, all of whom pitched in to help us. We owe a special debt of gratitude to Dr. Truman Coates who, ninety years ago, researched, wrote, and published a comprehensive history of his family.

Michael McNierney's knowledge of western history and enthusiasm for this project encouraged us to forge ahead. We are indebted to Mira Perrizo for her skillful editing and enduring patience. And we would never have gotten anywhere without our editor, Stephen Topping. He gently nudged us back on track when we strayed into peripheral and unproductive byways, brought his own extensive background in military history to bear on the innumerable problems that came up, and made sure that we did justice to the story of an intriguing human being.

W.J.D. Kennedy

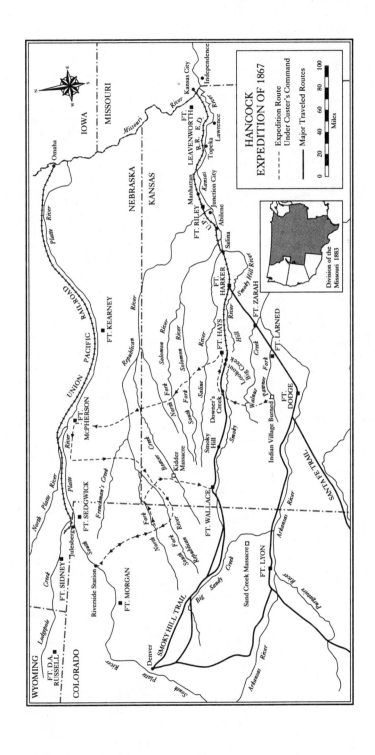

HANCOCK
EXPEDITION OF 1867

--------- Expedition Route
·········· Under Custer's Command
━━━━━━ Major Traveled Routes

Miles

0   20   40   60   80   100

Division of the
Missouri 1883

Introduction

Moses and Susanna Coates

IN THE SUMMER of 1717, Moses Coates, son of Thomas Coates of Bally-cater, County of Tipperary, and his wife, Susanna, daughter of Samuel Weldon of Gullacane, left Carlow, Ireland, bound for America and "a home free of secular bigotry and burdens of the Crown." Many years before, probably in the early seventeenth century, the Coates family had fled from England to Ireland, seeking to escape persecution of their Quaker faith. The name Coates appears in court records of 1661, when O. Coates went to see the chancellor to arrange for the release of friends (Quakers) from prison.

We do not know when either Moses or Susanna were born, but Truman Coates wrote that records exist in Ireland of their request, according to Quaker tradition, for consent of the meeting that they be married. On March 1, 1717, they were married in the meeting house in Cashiel, County of Tipperary, only a few months before they embarked for America. The minutes of the Haverford (Pennsylvania) monthly meeting of October 1, 1717, note that Moses Coates brought with him a certificate from friends in Carlow attesting to his good behavior. In March 1731, Moses Coates purchased 150 acres of land in the colony of Pennsylvania on the north side of French Creek, at its junction with the Schuylkill River, where he built a house and planted locust trees. Wolves were so troublesome that the sheepfold was built against the house for greater security. On winter mornings, the snow would be beaten down by the feet of wolves trying to get to the sheep. That winter, Moses trapped twenty-four beavers on the island across from where the town of Phoenixville now stands. A few other settlers lived in the area, some of whom had slaves. At first, the Coates family was apprehensive about the Indians who lived along French Creek but soon learned they were friendly. As the Indians died, one by one—until they all disappeared—they were buried at Green Hill and Black Rock. All signs of the burial sites, however, disappeared more than one hundred years ago.

Moses and Susanna had eight children, six of whom lived to adulthood. Moses and his sons James and Moses, Jr. continued to buy land in the French Creek area for the next twenty years. At that time, the Pikeland area was still an unbroken wilderness. When Moses died in 1761, his will included a bequest of six pounds a year to Susanna plus "the household goods that she brought with her and the new white Rug and the tea table and small Brindle Cow." The "goods and chattles" of Moses Coates of Chester County were valued at 239 pounds plus a great deal of valuable land. Moses and Susanna, who died in 1772, are buried in the Pikeland Friends Burial Ground.

The second child of Moses and Susanna, Samuel, Isaac Coates's great-grandfather, was born in 1718. He married Elizabeth Mendenhall in March 1743 in the East Caln Meeting House. Samuel and Elizabeth moved to land owned by Samuel's father near the village of Caln. Samuel and Elizabeth had four children, three of whom lived to adulthood. The minutes of the August 16, 1746, Caln meeting contain a complaint that Samuel Coates and others had gone to the house of Robert Miller in the night and abused Robert "by calling him many bad names." Samuel and Elizabeth are buried in the East Caln Friends Burial Ground. We do not know when either died.

Isaac's grandfather, Moses, Samuel and Elizabeth's child, was born in 1746. He married Hannah Musgrave in 1770. They had two daughters, both of whom died of consumption as young women. Hannah died of "a Nervous Fever" five years after their marriage. In 1777, Moses married Mary Vickers. Moses and Mary had eleven children, nine of whom lived to adulthood. Their eighth child, Moses, born in 1789, was Isaac Coates's father.

Like his Irish grandfather, who began buying real estate soon after he landed in America, Moses was fascinated with land. In 1805, he, his brother Isaac, and his cousin Moses Mendenhall took "a tour of the State of Ohio," looking for the ideal piece of property. The travelers made their way from Phoenixville through York, Chambersburg, Bedford, and Pittsburgh, and then north into the country along the Big Beaver River, where they found "almost everything necessary for a regular and good livelihood and a cheap and easy conveyance of produce to market." Flour could be shipped to New Orleans for one dollar a barrel, which was cheaper and safer than shipping it down the "dangerous Susquehanna." They rode the beautiful Ohio River down to Steubenville and then headed back home. Moses's journal is a meticulous accounting of the advantages and disadvantages of each of the regions he visited, based on a list of thirteen criteria including quality of land, available timber, limestone, water, wild game, serpents, fish, and tradesmen. Believing it best to follow the rule "measure twice before you cut once," Moses returned to eastern Ohio the next year, this time with his son Isaac and his son-in-law, John Way, but apparently he found "nothing yet sufficient to invite me from my Elysium at home." Instead Moses laid out the town of Coatesville on a large tract of land he owned in Chester County, named it, and became its first postmaster in 1812. He died in 1816 and is buried in the East Caln Friends Burial Ground, with Hannah and probably with Mary, although we do not know for certain.

In 1829, Moses, son of Moses and Mary, married Lydia Taylor, who was born in 1807. They had six children (one of whom died in infancy), including Isaac Coates. Lydia is the first of the Coates wives we know anything about. Howard Morton, her grandson, wrote in 1939 of his love for "that tall, finely featured Quaker lady." From that comment, we surmise that Isaac Coates was brought up with Quaker values, and, even though he seems to have left the Quaker faith later in life, his journal expresses with intense conviction the qualities of tolerance and compassion he learned from his mother and father. Isaac's father was a teacher and mathematician. We have his hand-written and hand-colored instructional booklet, dated 1815, entitled "Navigation." Moses died in 1844. We do not know where he is buried. Lydia, who died in 1878, is buried in the Chester Rural Cemetery. Since at least three of the children of Lydia and Moses lived in Chester, it is probable that Lydia moved there to be with them after Moses's death.

Isaac Taylor Coates

Somewhere along the way, the Coates's land holdings had been so dispersed among family members and sold off for cash that they no longer represented a substantial financial resource. Isaac Coates was born on March 17, 1834, and brought up in Coatesville in fairly humble circumstances, a problem he struggled with the rest of his life. Determined to study medicine, but without funds, he taught school in Delaware County until he had enough money to go to medical school. After receiving his M.D. from the University of Pennsylvania in 1858, he made several trips to England on the packet ship *Great Western*, of the Black Ball Line, as ship's surgeon, an experience he mentions in the opening pages of his journal. Isaac settled briefly in Louisiana but returned north at the outbreak of the Civil War to offer his services to the government. He was appointed surgeon on the steamship *Bienville* of the South Atlantic Blockading Squadron. In 1864, he was transferred to the frigate *St. Lawrence* and later to the gunboat *Peasta*. He resigned his position as fleet surgeon in September 1865 after receiving a commission from Governor Curtin of Pennsylvania. He then joined the Seventy-Seventh Pennsylvania Volunteers at Victoria, Texas, where he remained until the regiment was mustered out. Isaac was not alone among his brothers in choosing military service. Isaac's brother Joseph served in the First Regiment Pennsylvania Reserves. He was cited for gallantry at South Mountain and promoted to captain. At Gettysburg, he was wounded twice and promoted to major. Early in the war, their brother Amos became a hospital sergeant in the First Pennsylvania Reserves and was, according to family legend, poisoned by a female Confederate spy selling apples.

On March 22, 1865, Isaac Coates married Mary Penn-Gaskell, daughter of a wealthy Pennsylvania family and a descendent of William Penn. Their relationship remains something of a mystery. Although the marriage resulted in three children, two of whom died in infancy, Mary saw very little of Isaac, who was always off somewhere satisfying what he called his "thirst for adventure." Perhaps he needed to accept work wherever he could find it, but he seems to have chosen positions as far as possible from Chester, places like Texas, Georgia, and "Indian country." Furthermore, there is no evidence that Isaac was pining away for Mary when he was away; in fact, he never mentions her in his journal. We have a hint of what might possibly have been the cause of his frequent and prolonged absences in a comment by Howard Morton, who said in a 1939 letter that the Penn-Gaskells were a proud, aristocratic family and "austere, almost to the point of hardness." He added that "the Penn-Gaskell pride was a thing that the common chap did not swallow with pleasure," but protested that he loved his Aunt Mary "all the same."

From April 13 to July 17, 1866, Isaac Coates served as acting assistant surgeon with the United States Volunteers, Bureau of Refugees, Freedmen and Abandoned Lands at Atlanta, Georgia. In order to earn his pay of $100 per month, he was required to perform his duties "agreeably to Army Regulations and regulations of the Bureau of Refugees, Freedmen and Abandoned Lands." On February 18, 1867, Isaac Coates wrote from his home in Chester to Surgeon General A. K. Barnes to apply for a position as acting assistant surgeon with the United States Army, saying that he would be willing to go to the Territories for one or two years. He added that he had "a full set of instruments."

Since his request for an appointment had already arrived in the surgeon general's office when Isaac read in the newspapers about the impending Hancock expedition, he received a quick response to his application for duty. On March 7, Isaac signed a "Contract with a Private Physician," promising to perform the duties of medical officer "agreeably to Army Regulations in the Department of the Missouri or elsewhere and to furnish and keep in order, and accessible at all times, complete sets of amputating, trephining, and pocket instruments." For these services, he was to be paid $100 per month, or $113.83 "when performing services in the Field." He was also guaranteed return transportation to the place of contract when his service was completed. Four days later, Isaac boarded a train in Philadelphia for Chicago, St. Louis, Fort Leavenworth, and Fort Riley—following through Pennsylvania nearly the same course taken by his grandfather by foot and on horseback sixty-two years earlier.

War on the Plains

Plains Indians had been feeling the pressure of increased white travel and settlement long before 1867. By the late 1850s, it was already evident to white observers that buffalo were becoming scarce in some areas, but the Indians were still able to move on to other hunting grounds farther from white settlements and find the animals in ample numbers. Nevertheless, some Indian leaders were becoming alarmed about the presence of white men wherever they went: miners in the hills, settlers along the river valleys, freighters on the buffalo trails. As early as October 1859, William Bent, an Indian trader, wrote about the Kiowas and Comanches with remarkable prescience: "A smothered passion for revenge agitates these Indians, perpetually fomented by the failure of food, the encircling encroachments of the white population, and the exasperating sense of decay and impending extinction with which they are surrounded. ... A desperate war of starvation and extinction is therefore imminent and inevitable unless prompt measures shall prevent it."[1]

Except for an occasional skirmish, 1861 was quiet—a few warriors raiding isolated dwellings or attacking trains traveling through to Santa Fe, Denver, or Salt Lake City. These fights were not part of a pattern; they were individual raids by small groups of warriors out looking for a fight or some white man's goods. The next year, however, was different. From 1862 until the time, decades later, that the U.S. army had killed enough Indians to be able to subjugate the rest, war existed on the plains—usually as an intermittent struggle, with periods of savage fighting followed by temporary truces sometimes accompanied by peace treaties that never really stuck.

The switch from relative peace to general war seems, in retrospect, to have occurred quite abruptly. Suddenly, in the spring of 1862, Indians began attacking stagecoaches and stations along the North Platte, killing men and driving off stock. Militia troops were raised to protect the overland mail, but they were unable to catch any Indians. In May, Brigadier General Craig imposed martial law on the plains. Militia troops were dispatched to Fort Laramie and Fort Kearney. In the fall of 1862, Fort Halleck was established to protect travel through Wyoming. In November, a telegraph station on South Pass was attacked, and one man was killed.

On February 26, 1863, Denver's *Rocky Mountain News* called for troops to "wipe the treacherous vagabonds from the face of the earth." In July, after a series of raids by the Utes in western Utah, the First Colorado Cavalry, under Major Edward Wynkoop, caught a raiding party and killed from twenty to sixty Indians, with a loss of only one trooper killed and four wounded. In September, Governor John Evans of Colorado asked trader Elbridge Gerry to persuade the Sioux, Arapahos, and Cheyennes to come to a council of peace. When asked by the Indians what the governor wanted, Gerry said that the governor wanted the tribes to move to reservations and live like white men. LeRoy Hafen wrote that the Indians replied that they were "not reduced quite that low yet."

In the spring of 1863, the Indian agent for the Upper Arkansas region reported that many Indians were starving because there was little game in the area and no buffalo. White hunters had been killing buffalo by the thousands for their hides and tallow. By 1863 then, the buffalo, an essential element in the nomadic life of the Plains Indians, was already scarce along the Arkansas River.

In April of the next year, Grant was preparing to invade Virginia. Sherman was ready to begin his march to Atlanta. And Union forces were about to be engaged in some of the bloodiest fighting of the Civil War at the Wilderness and Spotsylvania Court House. The regular army was fully occupied by the Confederates and could give no help to the western territories. If military action against the Indians was going to be necessary in 1864, militia troops would have to carry the load.

After a relatively quiet winter, Colorado militia troops, sent out to recover what herders said were stolen cattle, burned five Cheyenne lodges. At about the same time, four militia soldiers and three Indians were shot near Orchard, Colorado, in a scrap over four mules. With the attention of civilian and military leaders in Washington riveted on the war to preserve the Union, western Indian policy was frequently made by volunteer officers and by territorial governors like John Evans of Colorado and Samuel Crawford of Kansas, who knew that their constituents favored killing Indians—any Indians—as the solution to the Indian problem. Phrases such as " attack any Cheyenne, friendly or hostile," "take no prisoners," and "kill all Indians, little and big" were common.

Lieutenant Eugene Ware, assigned to prepare Fort Cottonwood on the Platte River for a conference with Sioux leaders, was not sympathetic to peacemaking, convinced as he was that "Indians were a wild, bloodthirsty set of barbarians, and one half, at least, of them deserved killing as much as the wolves which barked around their teepees."[2] But traffic along the Platte continued to increase. Settlers counted as many as eight hundred ox teams a day passing their ranches, heavily guarded by armed civilians and soldiers.

In May, Major Jacob Downing and militia troops attacked a camp of Cheyennes in Cedar Canyon, north of the South Platte. George Bird Grinnell wrote that the Indians were not aware that there was trouble with the whites and the men were away, leaving only women and children in camp. Downing surprised the village at dawn, ordering his men to "commence killing them." Downing reported twenty-six Indians killed, thirty wounded, one trooper killed, and one wounded.

Also in May, Lieutenant Eayre and his Colorado volunteers discovered a large camp of Cheyennes near Fort Larned. White and Indian witnesses testified later that Lean Bear, approaching an officer with papers that proved the camp was friendly, was shot dead at the officer's command. In the fight that followed, twenty-eight Indians were killed. Four troopers were killed, and three were wounded.

Cheyenne, Kiowa, and Sioux warriors began raiding ranches and stage stations in retaliation for what they considered to be unprovoked attacks on them. Mr. and Mrs. Hungate and their two children were murdered by Indians on their ranch southeast of Denver. Their mutilated bodies were later placed on display in a store window in Denver, causing considerable unrest among the citizens. The Arapahos remained peaceful until troops at Fort Larned fired on Chief Left Hand as he approached the fort carrying a white flag. Well known to be friendly to whites, Left Hand was coming to the fort to help the soldiers negotiate with Kiowas for the return of stolen horses and mules. The soldiers missed their target, but the Arapahos promptly went on a raid up the Arkansas.

By July 1864, Indians were attacking emigrant trains, stage stations, and ranches along the Platte from Denver to western Nebraska. Travel

along the trail from Julesburg to Fort Laramie was limited to large, combined trains with sufficient men to protect them. Indian raids continued
across Colorado, Nebraska, and Kansas. By the middle of August, so
many trains and ranches had been attacked that even freighters, who had
continued to travel the Platte road after all stage traffic had ceased, cor-
raled their outfits and waited "for better times." On September 2, the
postmaster in Denver was instructed to forward to San Francisco all mail
bound for the East. The mail would then travel by ship down the west
coast, across the Isthmus of Panama, and up the east coast, to be delivered
some weeks later. West-bound mail was held in Atchison, Kansas, returned to New York, sent to San Francisco by ship, and then hauled east
by stagecoach to Salt Lake City and Denver.

Facing another winter of hunger, Black Kettle and other chiefs of the
Cheyennes and Arapahos brought their people to camp along Sand Creek
in southeastern Colorado. They had received assurances of government
protection from Major Wynkoop, and they also relied on a circular issued
by Governor Evans the previous June inviting friendly Indians to move
closer to military posts. Unfortunately for the Indians, Wynkoop was removed from command for being too accommodating to hostile Indians
and replaced by Major Scott Anthony, a disciple of Colonel John Chivington. Chivington and Anthony were encouraged in their strategy to
pacify the Indians by force by Brigadier General Patrick Connor, the same
General Connor who, according to Grinnell, would order his troops in
1865 to kill every male Indian over twelve years of age.

At dawn on November 29, 1864, Chivington, Anthony, and about
seven hundred volunteer troops attacked the Cheyenne village on Sand
Creek. As soon as the troops were seen approaching the village, Black
Kettle ran up a large American flag and a smaller white flag on a pole outside his lodge to show that the camp was friendly. Left Hand, the Arapaho chief friendly to whites, was one of the first to die. Black Kettle's
wife was shot off her horse but survived. Chivington later claimed that he
had killed five hundred Indians. Other estimates range from one hundred
to eight hundred dead, many of them women and children. The soldiers

also scalped and mutilated the dead bodies. A few days afterward, more than one hundred Indian scalps and severed limbs were exhibited in triumph between acts at a Denver theater.

Immediately after the Sand Creek massacre, the Cheyennes joined with the Sioux and Arapahos in a general war of revenge, attacking ranches and stage stations on the Platte and killing travelers and freighters along the Arkansas. A party of about one thousand warriors attacked and plundered Julesburg, Colorado, in the first week of January 1865, killing eighteen soldiers and civilians. In the same month, General Robert Mitchell and an expeditionary force of 640 cavalry and light artillery left Fort Cottonwood and headed west along the Platte in search of Indians. Ten days later the force returned to Fort Cottonwood without having caught an Indian, but with fifty soldiers who had to be discharged because of frozen limbs and other injuries.

In February, the Cheyennes, Sioux, and Arapahos made a combined raid along the South Platte. Julesburg was again attacked and plundered. Stage stations and ranches were burned, wagon trains captured, and the telegraph line destroyed along seventy-five miles of road. After a sharp fight with soldiers at Mud Springs, south of the North Platte River, in which both sides suffered losses, the Indians moved north to the Powder River country, between the Big Horn Mountains and the Black Hills, where they joined other bands of Cheyennes, Arapahos, and Sioux.

By mid-year, Indian depredations had become so serious a threat to travel and commerce along the vital North Platte road that General Grenville M. Dodge, commander of the Department of the Missouri, decided to attack the Indians in the Powder River country where their villages were concentrated. General P. E. Connor was given command of an expedition containing about 2,000 volunteer soldiers accompanied by 190 Pawnee, Omaha, and Winnebago scouts. In August 1865, they surprised a camp of about twenty-four Cheyennes and killed the entire party. Later, General Connor discovered and attacked an Arapaho and Cheyenne village of two or three hundred lodges. Many Indians were killed or taken prisoner, and 600 horses were captured. Connor's forces suffered only modest losses.

Since the enemy had taken significant casualties and had been through the shattering experience of losing a large village, the expedition could have been counted a success. However, two of Connor's senior officers, knowing nothing about Indians and fighting on the plains, committed a series of egregious errors that resulted in the loss of hundreds of horses and the near-starvation of a large number of troops. In early September, the command was attacked by a combined force of Cheyennes and Sioux under the leadership of Roman Nose, the Cheyenne warrior whom Isaac Coates would meet in April 1867. The troopers were short of food and had lost many of their horses but managed to fight off their attackers and continue their retreat up the Powder River. General Connor was held responsible for the debacle and relieved of command. Grinnell thought that Connor's greatest mistake was to assign primary responsibility for major portions of the expedition to officers who were ignorant of plains warfare. The army would repeat that mistake in 1867 and Isaac Coates would witness the consequences.

In mid-summer, Arapahos, Sioux, and Cheyennes, led by Roman Nose, raided along the Platte and engaged in a running battle at Platte Bridge, where Lieutenant Caspar Collins and more than ten of his men were killed. On the Smoky Hill road, peace lasted just long enough for the Butterfield Overland Despatch to make its first coach run to Denver in September. The Indians responded immediately to this new invasion of their vital hunting grounds by attacking stage stations and coaches of the Overland Despatch at Monument Station, Downer's Station, Chalk Bluff, and Big Creek. In November, Theodore R. Davis, reporter for *Harper's New Monthly Magazine*, camped by the ruins of Downer's Station a few days after it had been attacked and burned. Davis's own party was attacked at Smoky Hill Springs but was rescued by a company of soldiers "coming to bury us." October, November, and December were bloody months on the Smoky Hill.

General Sherman Assumes Command

In April 1865, the Civil War came to an end, Abraham Lincoln was assassinated, and Andrew Johnson became president of the United States. In May, after the Grand Review in Washington, Lieutenant General William T. Sherman bade farewell to his "bummers," men of the four corps who had followed him on the march from Atlanta to Savannah, and moved his family to St. Louis. His new command, the Military District of the Mississippi, extended south from Canada to Mexico and west from the Mississippi to the Rockies. His immediate problem was to prepare a strategy for dealing with the growing conflict between Indians and whites moving west, but he had other worries as well. The eastern half of the country, especially Washington, was absorbed in the battle between President Johnson and the radical Republicans in Congress over Johnson's moderate reconstruction program for the South. Johnson, like Lincoln, considered the southern states to have never left the Union. To the fury of the radical Republicans, who wanted revenge against the South, Johnson proposed to restore civil government to the southern states as quickly as practicable. As a consequence, Johnson was subjected to the foulest personal abuse by members of Congress and the radical press in an effort, ultimately successful, to cripple his administration. Even Johnson's Secretary of War, Edwin M. Stanton, conspired with the Republicans against Johnson. Stanton was the civilian superior of Sherman and Sherman's boss, Ulysses S. Grant.

The fight between the president and Congress over Reconstruction was a continuing threat that might at any time have overwhelmed the shrinking resources of the U.S. Army. In January 1867, Sherman wrote his brother, Senator John Sherman, of his fears that war would break out again in the South if Johnson were impeached and the southern states reduced to the status of territories. Command of the post-war army went to Ulysses S. Grant, who was made a full general—the first since George Washington—in recognition of his leadership of the Union armies in the Civil War. Having bestowed the title of General of the Army on Grant,

Congress immediately proceeded to slash the army's budget, drastically reducing the number of troops available for the dual purposes of keeping peace in the South and dealing with the Indian menace in the West. Grant's army was shrinking fast. Of the 1,034,064 volunteers remaining to be mustered out in May 1865, more than 800,000 had returned to civilian life by November. General Grant asked for a standing army of 80,000 but Secretary of War Stanton cut it to 50,000.

In the same few months, the public's opinion of the army had become sharply divided, as it always does after a war. With the defeat of the Confederacy, the military could no longer count on being enthusiastically acclaimed as the potential saviors of the Republic. On the contrary, even the diminutive army left after the massive reductions in force and cuts in military budgets was resented as too expensive. And military commanders had another problem. In the East, humanitarian groups turned their attention from abolishing slavery to protecting Indians from the army, which they suspected of following a policy of extermination. At the same time that westerners were howling for more soldiers to save them from the Indians, easterners were demanding that the Indians be treated more kindly.

Reponsibility for managing Indian problems was divided between the Office of Indian Affairs of the Interior Department, which was supposed to look after the interests of the Indians, and the army, which was charged with keeping the peace. As might be expected, the system worked badly. The army and the "Indian Bureau" were in constant conflict, harassing each other and making each other's job more difficult, and the Indians became the victims as they received conflicting messages from agencies of the same government. Widespread corruption in the Indian service made matters worse.

Out in St. Louis, General Sherman was trying to ignore the potshots from the East and, at the same time, convince the West that he was doing the best he could with the resources available to him. Sherman had another distraction as well. He was, with Grant, one of the two most admired public figures in the country and, therefore, the ideal catch for politicians who wanted him to be identified with their interests. Constantly fighting off efforts to bring him back to Washington to fill one position or another, Sherman feared being drawn into the maelstrom of partisan politics and rampant corruption. His friend and brother-in-arms, Grant, on the other hand, succumbed quickly and easily to political enticements and, by the middle of 1867, had joined with the radical Republicans.

The year 1866 opened quietly on the frontier. The ignominious conclusion of General Connor's Powder River expedition the previous fall had brought a temporary halt to the war along the Platte. The army made no more forays onto the northern plains that year and the Indians stayed away from the northern settlements, some moving into camp for the winter, others going south to raid the Kansas stage stations, where the fighting continued well into December.

This time, the war did not resume in the spring. The plains were so peaceful, in fact, that General Sherman and his brother John could make a wide sweep in the summer and fall through the area of Sherman's command, all the way to Fort Garland in New Mexico, and never see a "dangerous Indian." The Shermans had a delightful time, but their inspection tour did not provide them with an accurate picture of what the plains could be like when Indians were out looking for trouble. If they had been unlucky, they might have witnessed one of the occasional Indian attacks on stations and stage coaches on the Smoky Hill road or the Laramie road that took place during the time of their tour; instead, they traveled thousands of miles in peace. Sherman wrote John in October that the rumors of Indian troubles were "only accountable on the supposition that our people out West are resolved on trouble for the sake of the profit resulting from military occupation."[3]

During his summer swing of the West, Sherman saw with his own eyes what he knew to be happening but could hardly believe. Since the end of the Civil War, emigrants were heading west in a flood. His division was changing by the week, even by the day, as two railroads advanced west, sometimes laying track at better than a mile a day. A year earlier, Schuyler Colfax's party had performed the unheard-of feat of traveling the 635 miles from Atchison to Denver in four and a half days. A year after Colfax's trip, the Union Pacific Eastern Division (Kansas-Pacific) would reach Manhattan, Kansas. The overland mail terminus was subsequently moved west from Atchison to Manhattan, and, from then on, mail was carried to Denver by the Smoky Hill route. Meanwhile the Union Pacific, along the Platte, had reached Fort Kearney. As the two railroads proceeded west, they split Indian buffalo ranges into parallel strips. In addition the Overland Trail, along the Platte, and the Santa Fe Trail to the south, along the Arkansas, were carrying enormous volumes of stage and freight traffic. They also divided Indian lands into smaller strips, impeding the migration of the buffalo herds on which the Indian culture depended. The Indians watched their country being cut up into pieces. They were being squeezed from both the east and the west, where settlements along the Colorado front range had become large enough to block passage through the mountains from the plains. Settlers were also moving east onto the plains from communities along the Colorado foothills. The Indians were being pressed from all sides but had no place else to go.

In the spring, summer, and fall of 1866, small groups of Sioux warriors made occasional forays against isolated stations and on travelers, especially on the new, hated Bozemen Trail to the Montana mines. In December, Captain Myles Keogh reported from Fort Wallace, Kansas, that Cheyennes had attacked Chalk Bluffs Station on the Smoky Hill road and had killed some stock tenders. In the same report, he complained that the temperature had dropped to six below zero, and he could not build shelter for his horses because the nails he was waiting for had not arrived. Then, in December, the news reached St. Louis that the Sioux had wiped out Captain William Fetterman's entire command of some eighty men near Fort Phil Kearny on the Bozeman Trail.

Sherman reacted with fury and said some unfortunate things about exterminating all Sioux—men, women and children—which raised the hackles of humane groups in the East. On December 30, 1866, he wrote in a private letter to his brother, "I expect to have two Indian wars on my hands, and have no time for other things. The Sioux and Cheyennes are now so circumscribed that I suppose they must be exterminated, for they cannot and will not settle down, and our people will force us to it."[4]

Looking at his maps of the vast area included in the Division of the Missouri, Sherman knew that there was no chance whatsoever of protecting all the freighters, miners, and emigrants exposed to Indian attack anywhere they chose to travel on the plains. He had far too few troops. His only hope was to confine travel to the main roads, regulate the flow of traffic, and place detachments of troops at fortified sites as closely spaced as possible. The spacing was never close enough, as Isaac Coates would discover at Lookout Station. Wagon trains were required to follow strict guidelines as to organization, size, and number of riflemen. A similar system had been implemented on the Santa Fe Trail in 1865, using Fort Larned as the eastern end of a military escort plan.

To General Sherman, the difficulties of deploying a grossly insufficient force to protect a rapidly increasing stream of travelers, as well as the overland mail and railroad construction crews, were daunting enough. But he also had to cope with constant carping from the Indian Bureau about everything he planned to do. The bureau favored negotiation over military force in the hope that, through the use of peace commissions and other non-violent persuasive tactics, the Indians could eventually be persuaded to go to reservations set aside for them. Sherman had other, more immediate, problems, and he deeply resented the interference of the advocates of conciliation. His efforts to have the Indian Bureau transferred from the Department of the Interior to the War Department probably did not enhance his relationship with the agency.

In October, Sherman successfully fought off President Andrew Johnson's efforts to make him secretary of war. He knew his Indian problems would only get worse, but in November, his attention was again distracted by an order to go to Mexico as escort for the American minister to President-elect Benito Jaurez. He returned to St. Louis at the end of December to spend a few weeks at home and was then summoned to Washington.

Back in St. Louis, Sherman worked on plans for the spring campaigns. He had already asked that Major General Winfield Scott Hancock be as-

signed command of the Department of the Missouri, one of four departments within Sherman's division, now called the Division of the Missouri.
Hancock, called "Hancock the Superb" by General McClellan, had an exceptional record in the Civil War, and Sherman counted on him to bring
his leadership abilities to the busy territories of Colorado, Kansas, and
New Mexico. Hancock assumed his command in August 1866.

In January 1867, the newly formed Seventh Cavalry was at Fort Riley,
under the immediate command of George Armstrong Custer. Sherman
wrote his brother John that G. A. Custer was in his command and he was
"bound to befriend him." He also wrote that Custer was "young, very
brave, even to the point of rashness, a good trait for a cavalry officer."[5]
Sherman, like his subordinates, did not yet distinguish between cavalry
engagements in a conventional war and fighting Plains Indians, the greatest of all cavalry.

Sherman began 1867 with the prospect of renewed fighting with the
Sioux and Cheyennes in the spring amid unrelenting opposition from
many in the East to a military solution to the Indian problem. He, Grant,
and Andrew Johnson wanted a success in the new year—Sherman, because it was his duty to produce victories, and he always did his duty;
Grant, for both military and political reasons; and Johnson, because any
achievement would be better than the string of humiliations he was being
handed by Congress. Sherman and his field commander, Hancock, were
under tremendous pressure to plan and execute a campaign into Indian
country as quickly as possible—a plan that would, for the moment at
least, silence the critics and muffle the Indian Bureau.

In March, Sherman wrote Hancock that the Cheyennes, Arapahos,
and Kiowas

have assembled at or near our posts on the Smoky Hill, and on the
Arkansas, in numbers and strength manifestly beyond the control of their
agents, and have in manner and word threatened to interrupt the use by our
people of those roads. This cannot be tolerated for a moment. If not a state
of war, it is the next thing to it, and will result in war unless checked. I

therefore authorize you to instruct your commanding officers of posts on a recurrence of the same or similar cases, to punish on the spot; and I authorize you to organize out of your present command a sufficient force to go among these Cheyennes, Arapahoes, Kiowas, or similar bands of Indians, and notify them that if they want war they can have it now; but if they decline the offer, then impress on them that they must stop their insolence and threats, and make their conduct conform more nearly to what we deem right than was the case last year.[6]

Hancock, in turn, issued General Field Orders No.1, which read in part as follows:

It is uncertain whether war will be the result of the expedition or not; it will depend upon the temper and behavior of the Indians with whom we may come in contact; we go prepared for war, and will make it if a proper occasion presents. We shall have war if the Indians are not well disposed toward us. If they are for peace, and no sufficient ground is presented for chastisement, we are restricted from punishing them for past grievances which are recorded against them; these matters have been left to the Indian Department. No insolence will be tolerated from any bands of Indians whom we may encounter; we wish to show them that the government is ready and able to punish them if they are hostile, although it may not be disposed to invite war.[7]

Even though he must have shared Sherman's aversion to the Indian Bureau, Hancock made genuine overtures to agents Edward Wynkoop and Jesse Leavenworth, explaining the purpose of the expedition and asking them to accompany him on the trip "to show that the officers of the government are acting in harmony." Unfortunately for everyone, especially the Indians, Hancock's gesture toward unanimity did not mean that he trusted the agents enough to take their advice when a pivotal question arose of whether or not to burn the Indian village on the Pawnee Fork. His decision to burn the village caused him much trouble later on.

Although the army and the Indian Bureau disagreed strongly about methods for pacifying the Indians and moving them to lands where they would no longer be in direct conflict with whites, their policies may actually have been less at odds during Hancock's campaign than at any time thereafter. In a closing paragraph in his March letter to Hancock, Sherman set a standard for treatment of Indians by the regular army: "I have no fear that you or any other officer under you will kill or injure unresisting people of any race or kind, and will not suppose the case. But such an impression has got abroad." Although Sherman's attitude toward conducting war changed drastically later on, as the frustrations of Indian fighting became more apparent and more soldiers were killed and mutilated, this statement reflects his view of appropriate conduct at the time of the March expedition. He was confident that Hancock would understand what he meant and act accordingly. Although Sherman did use the word "extermination" at least twice immediately after the Fetterman massacre, he almost certainly did not intend to implement a policy of annihilation at that time.

Sherman and Hancock were still thinking in terms of fighting enemy soldiers—in this case warriors—rather than making total war against enemy civilians. Hancock did not set out to burn Indian villages, empty or occupied, nor did he plan to drive women and children out of their homes. In fact, one of the ironies of the Hancock campaign is that, however it went astray in execution, it began as one of the last of the conventional military campaigns in the West. After the burning of the Indian village in 1867, and the fierce fighting that followed in the summer, U.S. military policy toward the Indians became much more harsh.

The "Unnecessary War"

Toward the end of his journal, Isaac Coates bids a thoughtful farewell to the "major general commanding," as Hancock leaves Fort Hays for his headquarters at Fort Leavenworth. Isaac wrote that although Hancock did not use his usual common sense in executing his campaign against the Indians, he was not to blame for its failure because "the General had been sent out to do what could not be done." Regardless of whether the fault lay with Hancock or Hancock's superiors, Isaac thought the expedition caused a cruel, unnecessary, and fruitless war against Indians who might otherwise have remained peaceful.

He may have been correct. It is possible that the summer of 1867 would have been quiet along the Smoky Hill route if Hancock and the Seventh Cavalry had not embarked on the army's campaign of intimidation. It is also possible that the plains tribes had not been poised for a last effort to drive the white men off their hunting grounds, but rumors had the Indians ready to strike when the grass was up in the spring. In January 1867, Major H. Douglas, commander of Fort Dodge, wrote to General Hancock that he had been told by Kicking Bird, a Kiowa chief, that the plains tribes were planning to go to war. If, indeed, they were ready for battle, then Hancock merely pulled the trigger of a gun that was already loaded and cocked. Was "Hancock's War" a new and needless conflict? Isaac Coates certainly thought it was, but he also believed, wrongly, that the stagecoach line along the Smoky Hill had been "unmolested" for two or three years before the spring campaign.

Another member of the expedition, Edward Wynkoop, apparently thought along the same lines as Isaac Coates. Unlike Isaac, however, Wynkoop knew a great deal about Indians from his experience as an agent for the Cheyennes and Arapahos and as a former army officer and Indian fighter. On April 15, 1867, he wrote his superior in the Office of Indian Affairs in Washington, "I am sorry to say that the result of the expedition is disasterous. ... I am fearful that the result of all this will be a general war."[8] George Bird Grinnell, who had lived with the Cheyennes and knew them well, wrote bitterly in 1915 that Hancock had driven the Indians into war. Many contemporary scholars agree that Hancock started a war that need not have happened.

We will never know whether the Sioux and Cheyennes would have remained peaceful that summer if no organized expedition had entered the plains or if another officer who was more experienced with Indians had been in command. Hancock's fumbling and ill-advised decisions undoubtedly caused the Indians needless suffering, which infuriated Isaac Coates. The question remains, however, whether the plains tribes ever would have been persuaded to abandon their traditional lands and move to reservations without more fighting.

By November 1868, Sherman and Sheridan (who had replaced Hancock) were happy to commend Custer for attacking Indian villages on the Washita River, a battle in which many women and children were killed. Soon after, Sheridan made his famous remark to an Indian chief: "The only good Indians I ever saw were dead." Sherman wrote Sheridan in December 1868 that though he believed generals Sheridan and Hazen were able to carry out army policy, he wanted chiefs Bull Bear and Satanta killed before the generals allowed "any favors" to be granted to the tribes.

Sheridan intended to settle the Indian problem one way or another. Extermination was one viable possibility—but there was also another. He predicted it with chilling accuracy, in October 1868 when he said, "The object is to reduce the Indian tribes ... to such a state of submission and poverty as will cause for all time to come a permanent peace."

Winfield Scott Hancock

Historians writing about "Hancock's War" (a derisive title) have been highly critical of General Hancock's leadership of the March expedition. Some have gone so far as to cast him as a buffoon bumbling around Kansas with fifteen hundred men in tow, futilely pursuing uncatchable Indians and oblivious or indifferent to the suffering he was causing women and children. Some of the harsh criticism seems justified, but much of the rough treatment given Hancock can be attributed to the prejudices of certain writers. Champions of Custer, for example, will never forgive Hancock for supporting the charges brought against Custer that resulted in his court-martial. Indian sympathizers see Hancock as the willing, if inept, agent of a national military policy bent on extermination. Nearly everybody agrees that Hancock was unqualified to lead the expedition because he was inexperienced in Indian warfare. And most, but not all, writers assert that the expedition failed to meet its objectives. An odd note is that George Bird Grinnell, a friend and admirer of the Cheyennes who was outraged by the purpose and management of the campaign, cites as proof of its failure Hancock's inability to kill more Indians.

A broader perspective on these tragic events must take into account who the men involved were and what conditions and constraints affected their decisions. It is even possible that part of Hancock's bad press stems from journalists' propensity to knock statuary off their pedestals. And as one of the most admired generals of the Civil War, Hancock was indeed on a pedestal. Sherman, who knew Hancock well, went to great lengths to remove General Philip St. George Cooke, a veteran of western campaigns, from the command of the Department of the Mississippi in order to replace him with Hancock, who had no western experience at all. General Grant, who was not one to hand out unearned compliments, thought Hancock "the most conspicuous figure of the general officers who did not exercise a separate command. ... His genial disposition made him friends, and his personal courage and his presence with his command in the thickest of the fight won for him the confidence of the troops serving under him. No matter how hard the fight, the Second Corps always felt that their commander was looking after them."[9]

Hancock earned the respect of Grant and Sherman by his exceptional leadership throughout the course of the Civil War. He served with distinction in many of the most important battles, in several cases assuming command of a significant part of the action. He commanded brigades at Malvern Hill, the Second Manassas, and Antietam as well as divisions at Fredericksburg and Chancellorsville, where he successfully covered the Union Army's retreat as his division came under intense fire from three sides. President Lincoln rewarded his achievement at Chancellorsville by giving him command of the Second Corps.

Gettysburg, however, established Hancock's reputation as one of the best Union generals of the entire war. When Major General John Reynolds was killed on the first day of the battle, General George Meade sent Hancock to take field command of the federal forces, which were in danger of being overwhelmed by superior Confederate strength. Hancock rallied his men and held his position until the end of the day's fighting.

Just before nightfall, Hancock realized that Culp's Hill was not occupied by either side. He knew that if the Confederates got there first, they would threaten the entire Union line. Hancock thus ordered a division to secure the hill. After midnight that night, Meade and Hancock rode around the battlefield to assess the prospects for the next day.

On the second day of the battle at Gettysburg, Hancock had his best day of the war and, indeed, one of the best days of any general in the Civil War. He was an instrumental architect of the successful Union defense, moving from crisis to crisis, always in the right place at the right time. The climax of the three-day battle came on the third day when Major General George Pickett's divisions charged the Union center on Cemetery Ridge. Hancock's men faced and broke the charge. Though Hancock was wounded, he remained on the field, issuing orders from a stretcher. Commenting on Hancock at Gettysburg, Bruce Catton states he "was probably the best combat general on the Federal side ..."

By the time Grant and Lee met in the Wilderness in May 1864, Hancock had recovered from his wound and was back in command of the Second Corps. On May 10, he led all attacking Union forces against the Confederate lines. On the twelfth, the Second Corps charged the Confederate salient at Spotsylvania Courthouse, a place later known as the "Bloody Angle." Hancock and the Second Corps then moved south with Grant, sharing in the carnage of battles such as Cold Harbor. By the time the war ended, Hancock was known as one of the most brilliant fighting generals of the Civil War, admired especially for his courage, quick thinking, tactical skill, and decisiveness.

George Armstrong Custer

Of the two characters mentioned most frequently in Isaac Coates's journal, Custer and Hancock, a great deal has been written about the former and comparatively little about the latter. For that reason, the brief sketch of Hancock's Civil War career was given here. However, the controversial General Custer and his miscalculation on the Little Bighorn are the subject of so many authoritative studies, about equally divided between admirers and detractors, that one can select whatever interpretation one prefers. It seems superfluous therefore to offer another, which would in any case be drawn entirely from the work of other writers.

The Army Medical Department

From the moment he left Fort Riley, Acting Assistant Surgeon Coates was responsible for treating the illnesses and wounds of the men of Hancock's command. On the first morning of the march, he found himself treating troopers for frostbite, which was caused as much by inadequate equipment as by severe weather. The army took a long time to realize that the plains can be very cold in the winter and very hot in the summer. In the meantime, troopers wore Civil War uniforms on the march, lacking proper footwear and mittens for winter and without lighter clothing for the scorching Kansas summer. As a result, army surgeons like Dr. Coates had a great deal of practice treating frozen limbs and heat exhaustion, and the army lost many men by medical discharge or desertion.

Isaac Coates was able to find a position as military contract surgeon because, failing to learn from the lessons of the Civil War, Congress did not provide the army with adequate medical support. In a sweeping reorganization of the entire army, Congress had passed an act in July 1866 that, among many other things, established a meager Medical Department, composed of 1 surgeon general, 1 assistant surgeon general with the rank of colonel, 1 chief and 4 assistant medical purveyors with the rank of lieutenant colonel (and who were also assignable as surgeons), 60 surgeons with the rank of major, and 150 assistant surgeons with the rank of lieutenants of cavalry for the first three years, and, thereafter, the rank of captain. When the army was widely dispersed throughout the South and West, mostly in small detachments (239 posts in 1869), it needed a great many more medical practitioners than the 1866 law allowed. The solution was to employ contract surgeons for limited tours of duty, assigning them to units on campaign or to western posts like Fort Wallace. In 1866, 264 acting assistant surgeons were hired; 282 by 1868. Although some of the contract surgeons were conscientious and competent (Isaac Coates was commended by his superior, Dr. Lippincott, in a Medical Department circular), there was likely a wide range of professional ability within the group of doctors willing to accept positions that were temporary, often extremely uncomfortable, and sometimes, as in Isaac's case, downright dangerous. (And the salary was only one hundred dollars per month.)

The years immediately following the Civil War have been called the army's "Dark Ages." Yet the period of national neglect of the regular army and contempt for the soldiers serving in it actually lasted from the close of the Civil War until the beginning of World War I, when General John Pershing was given the task of overhauling the old army and preparing it for a modern war. He started with a military force that was, for that time in military history, as badly equipped, trained, and staffed as had been Sherman's soldiers on the frontier. Hancock's men marched out of Fort Riley into the snow and cold of the plains without proper equipment partly because the American people, as often happens after a war, had lost interest in the armed forces and demanded immediate and severe cuts in military budgets. Although fighting a war, the Seventh Cavalry was considered part of a "peacetime" army.

Robert Utley, in his thorough description of "army life on the border" in *Frontier Regulars*, gives a vivid picture of the deplorable housing—"dark, dirty, overcrowded, vermin-infested"—and the "bad food, badly prepared" that enlisted men were expected to endure for their tour of duty. A drawing of Fort Larned at the time shows caves in the hillside that served as barracks for some of the soldiers. Officers, as a general rule, lived a great deal better than the men. They had more freedom to improvise and more cash to purchase food to supplement the army diet. They were also permitted to hunt wild game and keep the meat for their own tables. Isaac Coates, who ranked as an officer, also enjoyed these privileges. It is evident from the writing of other officers in the Seventh Cavalry that he was fully accepted in the exclusive fraternity of officers and gentlemen.

Most of the men who needed medical attention suffered from disease or accidents, rather than wounds incurred in battle. The connection between sanitation and disease prevention was only vaguely understood.

Water fouled by human and animal waste was often used for drinking and cooking. Moreover, the causes of infection and effective methods of treatment were virtually unknown. Army surgeons on the frontier had to deal with all the ailments present in civilized societies at the time, but the year 1867 was an exceptional challenge for two reasons—cholera and scurvy. Cholera, highly contagious and often fatal, broke out in epidemic proportions in army posts across the West, including Fort Wallace, where Isaac Coates served in the summer of 1867. At that time, the cause of the disease was still a mystery.

The causes and prevention of scurvy, however, had been generally understood for years. It was known that soldiers, or sailors, fed on meat—salt pork, beef, or bacon—and bread, the usual army diet, could come down with scurvy. It was also known that green vegetables could prevent it. But green vegetables were not readily available. In the early 1870s, some post surgeons tried, with modest success, to persuade post commanders to plant gardens where vegetables could be grown for the garrison. In the absence of fresh vegetables, some surgeons insisted that wild green plants like lambs quarters, wild garlic, wild onion, and watercress be collected to supplement the troopers' diet. While rarely fatal, scurvy was a particularly nasty disease that could seriously debilitate victims and expose them to other, more serious diseases. Soldiers suffering from advanced stages of scurvy could actually reach into their mouths and remove sound teeth from their gums with their fingers. Severe ulcers could develop in scurvy victims, destroying tissue in the mouth, throat, and tonsils. Isaac Coates speaks of treating men with scurvy at Fort Hays in May 1867 and of waiting for anti-scorbutics—fruits and vegetables—that might never arrive.

A Note on Military Rank

Military rank in the post–Civil War army is inevitably confusing for modern readers and writers. Part of the confusion arises because during the Civil War the Union had maintained two armies—a regular one and a volunteer one. Some officers from the regular army were also assigned commands in the volunteer army, often at a higher rank. Brevet rank, adopted by the United States from the British military, further complicates the matter. Brevet rank was conferred for various purposes, but it was best known as a temporary or honorary commission, often for meritorious service. During the Civil War, these brevet grades were bestowed generously.

So an officer who remained in the army after the Civil War may have held as many as three different ranks. As it is beyond the scope and needs of this project to attempt to sort them out, I have left unchanged the ranks by which Isaac Coates addressed or referred to his colleagues.

Primary Sources

Even though Hancock's expedition was the first major offensive against the Indians to be mounted after the Civil War, only two news correspondents went along to cover the campaign. For some reason—perhaps because other, more exciting events were taking place elsewhere in the world or because newspaper publishers, like the American public, had lost interest in military affairs—the international corps of war correspondents who had followed the Civil War armies quickly disappeared. Although the two writers who did go on the march were experienced and skillful reporters, eyewitness reports about the spring expedition are so scarce that the writer of western history is limited to the observations of just a few individuals, some of whom had an obvious stake in the way highly controversial events were portrayed to the public. Isaac Coates, on the other hand, contributes his own, quite different, perspective.

Theodore R. Davis, one of the two journalists who accompanied Hancock in April and May 1867, was a writer with *Harper's New Monthly Magazine* and also an accomplished artist. He had made an exciting journey by stagecoach from Atchison to Denver along the Smoky Hill road in November of the previous year, nearly being killed by Indians on the way. He was credited with shooting an Indian while assisting in the rescue of a beleaguered ambulance during a fight at Smoky Hill Springs.

The other journalist was Henry M. Stanley, special correspondent for the *St. Louis Missouri-Democrat* newspaper. Stanley, of "Dr. Livingstone, I presume?" fame, overtook the expedition on the Saline River in March and remained with the cavalry until November. His faithful renditions of the speeches delivered by General Hancock and the Indian chiefs are frequently used as primary references by historians, as are his colorful descriptions of the people and places he observed on his travels across the American West. Stanley's accounts are accurate as far as they go, but the reader must be careful about his editing of the material. He leaves out small parts of speeches and, sometimes, entire sections of dialogue, whether through selective editing or because his sources were incomplete, it is impossible to say. Stanley had his own, clearly articulated prejudices about native people, which he demonstrated later on his notorious expeditions in Africa. So far as the American Indian was concerned, his sympathies lay with the mound builders, now departed, of the Mississippi Valley, whom the "savage and implacable" nomads now occupying the continent had replaced. He felt the latter could expect "no other fate than that of extinction."[10]

Two other members of the expedition, both army officers, also documented their experiences. George Armstrong Custer wrote an engaging, yet not always accurate, book about his life on the plains. He and his wife, Libbie, also exchanged letters that provide much useful information about the summer of 1867. The other officer was Captain Albert Barnitz, whose correspondence with his wife, Jennie, has been published in a volume edited by Robert Utley. For anyone who wants to know what it was like to be an officer in the post–Civil War United States cavalry, this is the book to read. One other invaluable source is the official record of the Interior and War Departments, contained in a report to the House of Representatives by the president and hereafter referred to as "Document #240."

Isaac Coates was present at one of the formal councils between General Hancock and the Indian chiefs. His journal quotes the speeches of Hancock and Tall Bull that he witnessed. He also presents speeches by Kicking Bird, Little Raven, and, especially, Satanta because he admired their oratorical skill and thought their addresses should be preserved for future generations. Undoubtedly, Isaac used transcripts of conferences that he found in the army's official reports, presumably in the form published in Document #240, to record these other speeches.

A valiant attempt has been made to track down all of the classical references that Isaac sprinkles throughout his journal. A few remain undiscovered, either because his handwriting is sometimes hard to decipher or because his knowledge surpasses that of the standard references. Undoubtedly, Isaac Coates carried around in his head most of his literary quotations, but he may have added a few later when reviewing his diary notes and preparing to write his journal. In an effort to avoid citing the obvious, and patronizing the reader, no effort has been made to explain references to the Bible or to the plays of Shakespeare.

Monday, March 11, 1867

It had been a long day. Isaac Coates had left Chester that morning, filled with anticipation about the adventure ahead of him and hoping he had made the right decision in joining the army. He knew about the Fetterman massacre of the previous December, but he had served as a surgeon in the wartime navy and the postwar army, and he was not a timid man. He had a long way to go—Philadelphia, Pittsburgh, Chicago, St. Louis, Fort Leavenworth, and, finally, Fort Riley, where General Custer and the officers of the Seventh Cavalry were waiting to meet their new surgeon. The night train for Chicago pulled out of the Philadelphia station, crossed the Schuylkill, and headed west toward the Alleghenys. Just a few days after he walked down the steps of his front porch in Chester, Isaac had traversed the civilized eastern third of the country, crossed the frontier, and entered a war zone. Five days later, he was in a tent, trying to sleep on frozen ground covered only by what he bitterly complained was inadequate bedding for a cold winter night on the plains.

On that same Monday, Hancock had just sent off a letter from his headquarters at Fort Leavenworth to Edward Wynkoop, agent for the

Cheyennes and Arapahos, which read in part: "My object in making an expedition at this time is to show the Indians within the limits of this department that we are able to chastise any tribes who may molest people who are travelling across the plains. It is not our desire to bring on difficulties with the Indians, but to treat them with justice and according to our treaty stipulations, and I desire especially in my dealings with them to act through their agents as far as practicable."[11] He went on to invite Wynkoop to accompany him on the expedition.

At Fort Riley, rumors of an impending campaign had been circulating for weeks, although, as Captain Barnitz wrote on Monday, March 11, from Fort Harker, it was not yet clear which Indians they would be going after or why.

Eleven days later, Isaac Coates arrived at Fort Riley with barely enough time to meet his fellow officers and assemble the arms and equipment he would need on the march. The first night was "wretchedly" uncomfortable, but Isaac learned fast. In a few days, he had scrounged up the gear he needed to cope with the cold, wet weather and was making perceptive, analytical, and sometimes humorous observations about life in the cavalry.

The Journal

ONE

The Journey West

It was about the first of March 1867, that I noticed in the papers an account of an intended expedition against the Indians of the Plains. At that time, I was enjoying the quiet of domestic life with no thought of an immediate peregrination anywhere. With the world of waters, with all its sublime and terrible realities, as well as with its calmer beauties, together with the thousand and one stories and romances connected with it, I was more familiar than 99 in every 100 that dwell on Terra Firma for "I have been down to the sea in ships." I have been once across the Atlantic Ocean in the New York and Liverpool packet ship *Great Western*, Captain Ferver, and three times in the good ship *Manhattan*, Captain Tom Dixon. I have been two years in the Blockade during the Rebellion on board the steamship *Grenville*, first with Captain Steedman, now Admiral, and afterwards with Captain Mullaney, now Commodore. All this aquatic travel, paradoxical as it may seem, had not quenched my thirst for adventure. The news that a great Indian expedition was to be set on foot awakened in my mind the slumbering visions of wildlife and thrilling incidents in the Far West which the perusal of Irving at first ignited years before.[1] What Fairyland is to Childhood, Irving had made the Far West to me. To look out on the boundless prairie, to see a wild savage Indian, to hunt the buffalo, to chase the antelope, to shoot the deer, inspired in my breast a passion as irrepressible as that which the fabled wealth of the New World awakened in the avaricious heart of the fiery Spaniard. And then to my mind, this expedition seemed to offer facilities for seeing the Plains that might not be again presented in years, for the U.S. troops, in pursuit of the Indians would traverse the whole country, east, west, north and south. Wherever the savages would go, it was to be presumed the troops would go also. To follow the troops in an expedition like this would offer facilities for seeing every beat of the Plains. Here was an incalculable advantage over travellers who could see and know nothing of the Plains except what was in sight of the stage road. My mind was at once made up to go if possible. An application to the War Department at Washington was answered in three days with an appointment in the Medical Department of the U.S. Army and orders to proceed to Fort Leavenworth, Kansas and report to General Madison Mills, Medical Director of the Department of the Missouri.

For some reason, perhaps because he thought it was an unnecessary detail, Isaac Coates does not mention that he had already submitted an application for an appointment when a vacancy should become available and had been accepted. He gives the impression that the War Department was even more efficient than it actually was. However, even though the groundwork had been prepared, a response of three days is impressive.

It would be paying a poor compliment to the magnificent territory lying between Philadelphia and Leavenworth to pass it in silence. No 1,200 or 1,500 miles in our country can be traversed without exciting in the mind of the traveller both wonder and admiration. We must essay a laconic sketch of the three days journey from the East to the West.

It was about midnight on the 11th of March, 1867, that I caught the last glimpse of the Schuylkill as the iron horse screamed his goodby to Philadelphia and dashed away westward over the Pennsylvania Central. Weary with the day's fatigue, I soon fell asleep, but my slumbers were frequently disturbed by the "rich Irish brogue" and the "sweet German accent" together with the high-keyed notes of a half-a-score of babies of different nationalities, each yelling in its particular linguistic squall. Oh! Morpheus for a Lethean nectar that every soul might quaff thee,[2] a libation, while I invoke "tired nature's sweet restoric balmy sleep."[3] This was my unanswered prayer.

I was on the immigrant train which is very comfortable and which carries you for about half fare. It would be worth while for every western traveller, for once at least, to throw himself into and float along with the Gulf Stream of western immigration. It is a good place to study character, Irish, Welsh, Dutch, all the nationalities of Europe are represented. There is a good deal of hilarity on the wing, and there is always a chance to learn something, if you will. Besides the foreign element, you have the company of many good western merchants, sharp-pursed travellers who are ambitious to see the world, and our own substantial yeomanry who are enroute for their new western abodes.

The beautiful clear morning found us among the mountains. The face of the country, in valley and in mountain, is joyous with prosperity. Look out on the face of cultivated nature and behold the mighty potency and influence of the locomotive, the Hercules of modern civilization. As we were speeding along the canal above Harrisburg, solemnly impressed with the wonders of this progressive age, we chanced to pass a wrecked canal boat when a witty Irishman set the car in a roar by striking up "Pat on the Raging Canal." We are soon at the great bridge. This is the age of bridges, and the train, like a flock of geese in the air, skims the broad Susquehanna, whose aquatic tread, majestic as a queen's, moves on to the ocean, carrying in her liquid fingers the dew drops and sparkling water from the summits of the Alleghenies as a present to old Neptune.

The mountain scenery is sublime. The morning sun gilds the fleecy clouds hanging above their summits. Such varied and exquisite colors. Ah! for the pencil of Parrhasius to steal them away.[4] For a while, we dash along the Susquehanna, then taking the beautiful Juniata, we follow for miles and miles its tortuous course amidst the wildest and most exquisite scenery, mountains rising over mountains and extending away in billowy succession until lost in the sleepy azure of the dim distance. The mountains are Nature's own imperial palaces. The Red Man once boasted these his home, but long since, his bark canoe that darted o'er the waters of the bright Juniata and broad Susquehanna has rotted on shore. His bow string is broken, his hatchet buried, his campfire is extinguished, and he has passed from the earth; and his papoose—whose lullaby was the liquid notes of the mountain cataract—has grown old, died and layed his bones in a strange land, where the sun sets beyond the great Father of Waters. And to indulge the imagination a little, the spirits of the departed red men have come back to earth to lament the loss of their fatherland. And their sepulchral voices from the rock-ribbed mountain gorges declare with Macbeth that:

> Life's but a walking shadow, a poor player
> That struts and frets his hour upon the stage,
> And then is heard no more: it is a tale
> told by an idiot, full of sound and fury,
> Signifying nothing.

No vestiges remain of his former hunting grounds. The white man has cleared away the forests, or usurped them, and grazes his flocks and herds where the deer once fed, and the panther made his lair. There is scarcely a mile along the railroad from Philadelphia to Pittsburgh that is not alive with the active industry of the white man. Where the wigwam stood, sending the curled smoke from burning faggots to the clouds, the farm house now stands warmed by the anthracite. Where stood the wilderness, the cornfield now smiles with its golden yield. From the valley to the very summit of the mountain, is dotted with the abodes of civilized man; and towns and cities line the iron highway from the Delaware River to the Ohio. It is a glorious sight to see the hardy yeomen carving out from the wild domain their beautiful farms. Here the Common People live—the jewels of the nation—the backbone of the country.

Reaching the base of the mountains our racing locomotive was taken off, and two iron draught horses attached, and away they go up the mountain side, panting and puffing, but they are equal to the task. I take the rear platform of the last car, in order to have a better view—the sight is worth a voyage across the Atlantic. The scenery varies at every turn, now wild and beautiful, now sublime and terrible. As you ascend, the eye wanders to the frightful depths below, and from almost the very summit of the mountain you look down to its base as from the top of a pyramid, and the head grows dizzy at the prospect. Great rocks dwindle into pebbles, giant trees to twigs, and the yawning chasms show like the creases in the palm of the hand.

Away the iron horse dashes with a wild and reckless career, now ascending now descending the mountainside, dashing around the shortest curves, whirling along the very edge of dizzy precipices, where ugly rocks jut out and wild waters dash and splash in their yawning channel away beneath us. Amid all these dangers, we are leaving the mile posts every two minutes, and once we passed three mile posts in four minutes. It is well for us the iron horse is sure-footed. Suppose he should stumble!

What a mote in the sunbeam is man when compared with the mountain! The very thought is calculated to take the pride and vanity out of him; yet though a speck when placed beside it, he is greater than the mountain, he has conquered it, triumphs over it, in majesty and might, as the viewless winds lord it over the oaks of the forest. In the engineering skill displayed here, we have a forcible illustration of the triumphs of man over nature. "Nothing new under the sun" says Solomon. What a stagnant period that must have been in the world's history! If the ancient Hebrew were living today to see the iron-horse climbing the mountain—dragging its ponderous load, or speeding like a bird—he would recall the expression. What children those ancient ancients were! Children, but grown-up children; dreaming dreams instead of thinking thoughts; feasting the mind with Lethean draughts of faith instead of exercising it with investigation. In every element for the amelioration of mankind, for the advancement of human progress, they are no more to be compared with us of this day than a mouse with an elephant. If they were with us in this period, they would be overwhelmed with our inventions, our liberty, our morality, and would fly for a congenial element to Utah.[5] I would not give our own Scott and Felton, those great railroad kings, for all the dreaming old fogies of antiquity.[6] Would'st thou, reader? But this is moralizing. A half a night's detention in Pittsburgh and we bade it adieu next morning at 7 o'clock. What a begrimed sooty face it wears! Though it has no smile on its face, its heart is warm with friendship; and we must look at it as Desdemona looked at the black face of the Moor when she "saw Othello's visage in his mind."

At 8 o'clock we had exchanged the noise and smoke of Pittsburgh for the still small voice of nature, with clear blue sky and lovely scenery along the beautiful Ohio; the belle rivière of the French missionaries, who were the first evangelical pioneers to launch their light canoes on its picturesque bosom, and the Ohi-o-lee-pee-chinn, or Ohio-lepechin, of the Indians, both sweet and musical names meaning the River of Beauty. It boasted but an unpretending flood, yet numerous messengers of commerce were seen gliding along over its quiet bosom. How often on the great stage of travel the scenes shift. The iron horse soon quits the Ohio valley, dashes in among the hills, leaps the Beaver, and, before the murmur of its waves has died away, we snuff the breezes of the Buckeye State. What an eloquent tribute to Labor is this state! Within the recollection of men still living it was a savage wilderness. Yet labor, despised labor, that is shut out of the mansion that it builds, that is denied a seat in the coach it made, that is often forbidden to eat off the table it framed, that receives for its share the husks of the corn and the chaff of the wheat that it produced—labor that is shorn of respectability and ostracized by society—labor, the mighty magician, metamorphosed this wilderness into a garden spot.

Who shall lawfully despise labor or degrade it, when it is the parent of almost every necessity, every comfort and luxury the world now enjoys or ever did enjoy? How would the aristocratic, church-going, Bible-reading, God-fearing, exquisites have their delicate sense of pious propriety shocked, should they see a painting of Christ representing him as a Carpenter with a box of tools in one hand, and a saw and a hatchet in the other, showing in himself the respectability and dignity of human labor, in which he was engaged from early manhood, perhaps, until he was thirty years of age. "Is not this the Carpenter, the son of Mary?" we read in St. Mark, Chapter 6, Verse 3. So much for labor. Let it never be driven forth with the curse of Cain on it. But if the world will do this, then let the world know that Heaven can furnish proofs of its respectability.

We passed through a beautiful farming district today (which impelled me to write the foregoing thoughts on Labor), where no more than fifty years ago, three uncles of mine settled in the then wild woods and before even a garden spot could be cultivated trees had to be cleared away, while on every side, wild animals, the panther, the bear and the wild-cat were disputing their possession. Now besides the cultivated farms, towns and cities dot the whole face of the country and the population now will almost equal the number of trees then; plenty looks out from every acre, and every town and city sends forth a smile of prosperity. Wonderful is the progress of the age, particularly in our country! And no less wonderful is the magical power of intelligent labor.

We reached Chicago in 23 hours from Pittsburgh, and were glad to have a few hours to rest and see the wonderful city. The mind is bewildered in contemplating the unprecedented growth of this place. What a miracle of a place is this Chicago—this city by the lake. It is sprung forth like a mushroom in a night. But a swamp a few years ago! Now it boasts hundreds and thousands of souls! What whirl of business! What a commerce with the lakes! Its universal comforts—its ten thousand luxuries—its great broad streets—its avenues of pleasure, its gigantic business and public buildings—its palacial edifices. With what restful ambition it spreads out its metropolitan wings! Is Chicago to be the London of America? We are accustomed to say that New York must be because she has the sea, but all the greatest cities of the world have been inland. Witness in ancient times Babylon, Nineveh, Zaalbec, Palmyra, Persepolis, to mention no others: in modern times, London, Paris, Peking. I made a visit to one of the public schools and found Chicago far in advance of the Fifteenth Amendment, for since 1862, there has been here no discrimination whatever on account of color, and this from the primary to the high school. Is the East behind? Or is the West ahead? How is it?

At 10 A.M., we were hurled away from Chicago on the St. Louis Express and were soon at sea on Terra Firma; shall I express it so? For the

wide prairies are flat and boundless like the ocean—the eye extending its
unobstructed gaze on every side to the distant horizon. The iron horse,
like a swift racer on a fine course, careers away measuring the leagues with
a frightful velocity. Towns and cities line either side of the iron highway,
and elegant farms checker the bosom of the broad plain. After hours of
the flat prairie, we reach a point where the land rolls up in successive un-
dulations, like the smooth billows of a summer sea. The whole face of nature here is an agricultural poem or painting, which you will.

And this is the home of our martyred President. I think of Springfield
as the Mahometan thinks of Mecca. Lincoln was one of Nature's Noble-
men! He had in an eminent degree what his latest, most laconic, and best
biographer, Charles H. Hart LLB, expresses so finely "the greatest of
goodness." Lincoln—Thou great high priest of Liberty, "While the tree of
freedom's withered trunk puts forth a leaf, even for thy touch a garland let
it be—Thou freedom's Champion, and the people's Chief—our new born
Washington—with reign, alas! too brief."[7]

There are two things that must particularily impress the mind of every
traveller as he whirls along over the western railroad. One is the incalculable advantages of railroads; the other is the work of the Common People. The railroads are the very soul of our national prosperity, and, next to
the press, the greatest civilizers in the world. But for these, this great state
would today have had a territory with a wild physiognomy instead of a
cultivated face. Prairie-grass would have fed the antelope and buffalo
where the richest cornfields in the world are now cultivated. It must be a
tortured logic indeed that will induce men to vote against appropriations
for the construction of the great continental iron highways. Without these
roads, the interior of our great country must for years remain as unprof-
itable as an island in mid-ocean without commercial communication with
the rest of the world. Let us have all the railroads we can. If the companies
grow "alarmingly" rich, let it be so; they deserve to be rich. They enrich
the nation and benefit every citizen from the greatest to the humblest.
Why shall they not, after being a blessing to the country, enrich themselves Croesus-like, if they wish.[8] As for the Common People, who shall
speak their praises? These hardy pioneers, who have carved great states

out of the wild domain, that have transformed the wilderness into the loveliest abodes for civilized man, that have made the hills rejoice with abundant harvest, covered the valleys with fattening herds, dotted the whole country with towns and cities exhibiting all the comforts and elegancies of a refined civilization. These are the pillars of the state—the honest men, the true, pure-hearted women—in their working attire they exhibit the finest aspect of human nature.

What a contrast between these and "the best society" of our great cities. Look at the enervated, sentimental fop who "entertains a score or two of tailors" with his fancy kids and his little cane and a whiffit at his heels— the better half of the twain—strutting like a peacock. What an insipid thing is he when compared with a western farmerboy, of whom Lincoln and Grant and Sheridan and scores of others are glorious specimens. And, as for the city wife, reared in idleness and luxury, taught to despise the very name of work, what a poor figure—when weighed in the balance of worth—she would make, with all her glitter, by the side of one of these daughters of the common people. Who shall apply the satiric lash hard enough to the old mothers of these city-pampered snipes for having given them so vicious an education? Who have taught them to be proud, envious, deceitful—"to lie with such grace"—to proclaim their highborn connections while they are of the scum, and their fabulous wealth when they can just "make both ends meet." In such a social college do they graduate. But the iron horse speeds on, darkness overtakes us and we reach St. Louis in the night.

This biting denunciation of the "city wife" may be more focused than it appears. Isaac Coates's wife, who is never mentioned in any of his writings, was a direct descendant of William Penn, and a member of a family that, as noted in the Introduction, was described by Isaac's cousin, Howard Morton, as "proud, aristocratic ... austere to a point of almost hardness."

St. Louis will prove another marvel to the traveller who has not before visited it. Its memory is still fresh with its frontier history, which seems but the other day, when it had the most motley population, Americans,

French, Creoles, half-breed Indians, Mississippi boat men, fur traders, trappers and hunters, together with representative Indians from all the tribes on the Plains. The forests around the city where the bear and panther were then hunted, have been cut away, and the prairie, where the buffalo and antelope fed, are now grazed by herds of cattle and sheep. The quaint old French appearance of many parts of the city has disappeared and, instead of a few winding streets along the crooked river, magnificent avenues lined with elegant mansions, the abodes of wealth, intelligence and refinement, stretch away for miles in length. More than half the population is of foreign element, and Germans, the most thrifty, industrious, intelligent, and best of our foreign immigrants, meet you here on every side. I spent Sunday evening in a German lager beer garden where both sexes came to enjoy themselves. So I sat watching those cheerful, happy people, their every action seemed to say "wine, wit and beauty still their charms bestow, light all the shades of life and cheer us as we go." These Germans are philosophers. They enjoy life. They make the most of this existence—lager and music in the next being uncertain, perhaps not even a meerschaum.

It is a long and most interesting day's journey from St. Louis to Leavenworth. No American can traverse the wonderful state of Missouri without feeling a laudable pride in its grand future. Its territory is great enough for an empire, and its mineral wealth beyond computation. It has over 41,000,000 acres, half of which is rich prairie, the other half heavily timbered. The Mississippi alone gives it 500 miles of water navigation, and the Missouri, extending to the very heart of the state, furnishes with its tributaries more than 1,000 more. Numerous sulphur chalybeate and petroleum springs abound, and the famous Bryce's Spring on the Maugua discharges daily 10,000,000 cubic feet of water and over, drives a large flour mill and runs away in a creek 42 yards wide. The geology of the state is so full, as to be able to furnish an almost complete geological cabinet. The coal area of this state covers between 25,000 and 30,000 square miles, promising an annual supply of 100,000,000 tons for at least 1,300 years. It has mountains of almost pure iron; and within the locality of Pilot

Knob and Iron Mountain alone, it is estimated that 1,000,000 tons per annum can be profitably manufactured for the next 200 years.

Along the track of the railroad, a constant variety is presented to the eye of the traveller. Here he beholds a magnificent farming district with all the cereals growing luxuriantly. There the hills and valleys covered with cattle and sheep exhibit a stock-raising district. Now he exchanges the cultivated fields for miles and miles of wooded country where finer timber than that destroyed by the pioneer now often finds its way into our shipyards. Again his eye is delighted with magnificent orchards and flourishing vineyards, and thus from St. Louis to Leavenworth.

On my arrival here, I was not long in finding General Mills, the Medical Director, a doctor of the Far West, and a very businesslike, straightforward, and decided man, but very courteous. After a delay of three days, I was greatly gratified on receipt of orders to report to General G. A. Custer at Fort Riley. After a day's journey in the cars over the Kansas-Pacific Railroad, I reached my destination.[9]

TWO

The March to Fort Larned

Impassable roads and high water prevented General Hancock from mounting his expedition on March 1 as he had originally planned, which was lucky for Isaac Coates, who would have found himself pursuing the expedition across eastern Kansas by stagecoach. Instead, Isaac and the various components of the force arrived at Fort Riley at the same time. Isaac and Battery B, Fourth United States Artillery, took the same train from Fort Leavenworth to Fort Riley on March 22. They were followed two days later by six companies of the Thirty-Seventh United States Infantry.

The officers whom Isaac Coates was to meet on the evening of March 22 had only been at Fort Riley for a few months themselves. The Seventh U.S. Cavalry was a new regiment, authorized by the Army Act of July 1866 and formed in September with headquarters at Fort Riley. Its commander was Colonel (Brevet Major General) Andrew Jackson Smith, an experienced Indian fighter and Civil War veteran. When Smith was ordered to take over the Military District of the Upper Arkansas, he retained the colonelcy of the Seventh, but field command fell to his deputy, Lieutenant Colonel (Brevet Major General) George Armstrong Custer. From then on, from February 1867 until July 1876, the Seventh Cavalry would be known as Custer's regiment, even though Smith ac-companied the Seventh on the Hancock Expedition and Custer received his or-ders from Hancock through Smith.

General and Mrs. Custer had arrived at Fort Riley in October 1866. Custer was pleased to have the assignment, which he secured in the rough and tumble competition for scarce army jobs that followed the mustering out of volunteer units after the Civil War. With fewer men to command in the new, much smaller post-war army, there were far more career officers seeking employment than positions available. Despite his brilliant record in the Civil War, Custer needed the intervention of his influential friend and patron, Major General Philip H. Sheridan, to obtain the appointment. Earlier that year, Custer, like many Union officers, had experienced a precipitous drop in rank and pay; in his case from major general in the volunteer army to captain in the regular army. He regained part of the lost ground when he was appointed to the Seventh Cavalry and promoted to lieutenant colonel. The title, "general," which he went by and dressed for, and which is still used today, came not only from his Civil War rank but also from the major general brevet he received in 1866, with Sheridan's help, in recognition of his Civil War service.

When he arrived at Fort Riley in the fall of 1866, Custer was looking forward to a challenging new command, and, perhaps more important in his eyes, he also saw before him, in the coming battles with the Indians, a chance for further recognition, promotion, and even greater glory.

I received a most cordial welcome on my arrival at Fort Riley from the post surgeon, Dr. William H. Farwood, an old friend. I was soon made acquainted with the officers of the 7th Cavalry, who were to be my associates in the Indian Expedition, and a splendid set of fellows they were. That evening was spent at General Custer's quarters where, for the first time, I saw this distinguished gentleman. The first thing I noted about the General was his laugh—the laugh is very indicative of character—which, soon after I had entered the room, burst forth volcano-like until the very windows shook. There was an intellectual vigor, a whole souled manliness and an indomitable energy represented in that laugh, that satisfied me with the man. His head and face reminded me of that of the Slavonic Noble. His accomplished wife was as agreeable as pretty. With other ladies we had a charming evening. The food for conversation was the Indian; and I was surprised to find with what fluency the ladies discussed the Indian Question, talked of war with the Savages and related Indian massacres until my mind was filled with horrible visions.

Fort Riley is one of the finest military posts west of the Mississippi. It stands on an elevation at the confluence of the Republican and Solomon Rivers which form the Kansas, commanding a spendid view of the country for miles in every direction. It was built in 1853 at a cost of half a million dollars. The magnesian limestone, a peculiar feature in the geology of this state, of whose peculiarities we shall speak hereafter, was used in constructing the buildings which are very capacious and comfortable. The Post stands 926 feet above the Gulf of Mexico and the elevation increases westward at the rate of about three feet to the mile; Fort Hays, 150 miles west, being nearly 1,500 feet above the Gulf of Mexico, and the same relative elevation continues on to the Rocky Mountains.

There is something inspiring in standing on an elevation like Fort Riley and looking out over the great state of Kansas. What a checkered and eventful history it has! I could hardly realize, as I looked eastward over the cultivated face of nature, smiling under the prosperity of free labor, that but a few years before, the soil had been fattened and the rivers crimsoned with human blood, in the wicked and vain attempt to curse the state with the blighting mildew of slavery.[1] When will men learn that wisdom is the principal thing; therefore get wisdom, and with all thy getting, get understanding? They had forgotten—how many now forget—that it is written: "In the sweat of thy face thou shall eat bread." It is not a little singular that the cruel bloody engine of war had to destroy the greatest of evils, Slavery, instead of moral forces. The "pen is mightier than the sword" says Bulwer, but the sword chopped the head off of Slavery—"give the devil his due."[2, 3]

As an illustration of the "quo animo" of the people of this state in regard to education, I will mention that the first act of the colony who founded Manhattan, a fine flourishing town east of this post, was to select a spot on which to erect a schoolhouse. Over the ground where, but a few years ago, Indian children played around their wigwams, 40,000 children are now attending the public schools. In 1719, the French government sent Monsieur Dutisue to explore this territory out of which this state has been carved; so that it then belonged to Louis XIV; later, Spain possessed it; then France again; until 1807, under Jefferson's administration, it was purchased with other territory for $15,000,000.

The Seventh Cavalry is often thought of as a cohesive unit operating as a regiment under the direct command of its leader, General Custer. In reality, the Seventh was rarely, if ever, together at one time and place in full regimental strength. When Isaac Coates joined the regiment at Fort Riley, all but four of its twelve companies, or troops, had already been assigned to duty at forts along the main travel routes further west. The regiment was spread out in small detachments, all of them at less than full strength because of desertions and disease, across the huge expanse of territory it was supposed to protect. The four companies of cavalry on Hancock's expedition were the last units of the Seventh Cavalry remaining at Fort Riley.

The expedition left Fort Riley on the 27th of March and camped for the night after a march of fifteen miles. It was composed of four companies of the 7th Cavalry, Battery B, 4th U.S. Artillery, and seven companies of the 37th Infantry, amounting in all to about 1,300 men. All this array of military, followed by the indispensable commissary train, a half mile in length, and pontoon trains, made a formidable appearance in the Indian Country. The weather was bitter cold when we started, and facing the chill winds by day and sleeping on the frozen ground by night, took away all the romance of travel. The first night was a terribly bitter experience. I had no idea of "roughing it" in the army. My experience of soldiering had been in the Navy. I missed the comforts, to say nothing of the luxuries, of an elegant state room on board ship. I was wretchedly provided with the necessaries for even a summer campaign, but this was winter, cold winter. I shared the bed and blankets of my companion-messmate, a senior officer, Dr. Lippincott. Though welcome as his bounteous generosity could make me, I felt a delicacy in sharing a narrow mattress and narrow blankets just in proportion as I had a demand for them. So, with the frozen ground—where the rough ice jogged me as if sleeping on a harrow—for a part of my bed and half protected by blanket, I passed a night that might have disturbed the slumbers of an esquimaux. It was a terrible school in which to receive instruction. Experience is the best of instructors because you never forget the lessons he imparts. I could not have forgotten this one, for it was engraved on the sensorium with the diamond of a Hyperborean god—an icicle.[4] But I was not the only sufferer. I pitied the poor fellows who came next morning at sick call with frozen toes and fingers. Some of the men were incapacitated for duty and went limping about with their hands and feet wrapped up, and so cold was the weather that for the first week, every morning added a few more to the frost-bitten list, until the ambulances were full. The sentinels on guard at night were usually the sufferers. The cavalrymen were compelled on the march to dismount and walk to keep themselves warm.

A single night's experience had surfeited me with Indian campaigning. But the iron grip of the government was upon me; there was nothing to do but make the best of it.

The culinary deportment of our "chefs" was no better than that of the upholstery. A little sugar and coffee, one ham, a few cans of vegetables, and a few pounds of "hardtack," a little mouldy, furnished the pantry. Almost frozen from the chilly night, I hobbled round at daylight next morning to get a mug of coffee. After begging so much of a log fire (belonging to some of the officers) as would be sufficient to boil my quart-mug of coffee, sat down after a half an hour, with half-frozen hands and feet and eyes running with tears from the smoke of the log fire to a breakfast as barbarous as the palate of a Patagonian could have wished.

Isaac Coates, some of his fellow officers, and all the enlisted men were miserably equipped for severe weather. However, General Custer's description of that first night in camp on Chapman's Creek was somewhat different from Isaac's. His letter to Libbie, his wife, speaks of enjoying the pleasant warmth of his Sibley stove and munching on ham, chicken, pickles, and biscuits, put up for him by Libbie before the march, in the congenial company of his five hounds Rover, Sharp, Rattler, Lu, and Fanny.[5]

On March 28, the expedition camped on Abilene Creek. Isaac Coates does not comment on accommodations at the camp site, but presumably they were like those of the previous night. Custer breakfasted on the remainder of Libbie's provisions, fried onions, baked potatoes, fried eggs, apple fritters, and warm bread, but he observed that the coffee was not strong enough. On the twenty-ninth, the command lost a pontoon bridge in the flooded, ice-filled stream. They camped on the Solomon River, where the officers dined on canned tomatoes and coffee. Many of the officers complained of being nearly frozen at night. Some said they were so cold they could not sleep. The weather continued to be intensely cold for the next several days. On April 3, Custer wrote Libbie from camp on Plum Creek that the day was the coldest yet and the officers were very uncomfortable. The elderly General Alfred Gibbs, who had joined the expedition at Fort Harker, was riding numb in the saddle, but Custer, with his phenomenal physical toughness, was "perfectly comfortable." Gibbs (brevet major general) was the senior major of the regiment and post commander of Fort Harker. He brought with him a squadron (two companies) of Seventh Cavalry under the command of Captain Albert Barnitz.

Our march continued along the Smoky Hill to Salina where the river deflects to the south and we part company to meet it again at Fort Harker where we arrived on the first of April, having marched in seven days no more than eighty miles. Remaining here until the 3rd, we again set out on the march over the Santa Fe stage route for Fort Larned which we reached on the 7th.[6] The cold weather had completely worn out the men, and the roads one day frozen rough and another day soft and heavy, had told severely on the cavalry horses and mule teams.

Isaac Coates says they had marched in seven days "no more than eighty miles," which was his best guess. Actually, the distance is about ninety miles. He must have meant six days, rather than seven.

THREE

Hancock's Grand Powwow
with the Indians

*Leaving Fort Harker on April 3, the expedition proceeded to Fort Larned by
way of Fort Zarah, a distance of about seventy miles. At Larned, one more company of the Seventh Cavalry was added to the force, bringing its total strength
to about 1,400 men. Henry M. Stanley gives a colorful description of the expedition on the march: "The whole of the journey from Zarah to Larned was
crossed with more circumspection and discretion than distinguished any of our
previous marches. The long commissary, quartermasters' and baggage trains
were kept closely together by detachments of cavalry. The infantry marched in
close, compact columns, and the veteran commanding officer was often seen casting glances of pride at the fine body of men under his command. The Seventh
Cavalry presented a good appearance, and their Colonel, General Smith, took
every occasion to drill them in cavalry tactics. When not practicing, they
marched in solid squadrons, the sight of which must have struck with terror any
observing bands of Indians."[1]*

*While the command marched with circumspection and discretion, General
Custer and his five dogs continued their regular morning assaults on the Kansas
rabbit population. On one occasion while he was riding his horse, Phil Sheridan, at full gallop, Custer's saddle came loose, and he was suddenly thrown full
length onto the prairie. As in another, even more dangerous, hunting accident
that Isaac Coates describes later in his journal, Custer was lucky not to have
been killed, either by the fall or by Indians.*

Fort Larned was the point at which the Indians were to meet General Hancock for a grand Powwow. This was to have been held on the 10th of April; but a violent snow-storm occurred on the 9th, which prevented it. The storm was of the most furious character; the driving gale from the northeast piled the snow about our tents like an avalanche; the storm raging from early in the morning until ten o'clock that night. Fortunately, we were in camp. Had we been on the march both men and animals must have perished. The thermometer of my romantic ideas of travel on the Plains was, indeed, now at zero. I could well appreciate, as I looked out of my tent over the desolate waste of snow, and saw the soldiers huddling around the great log fires, and the poor beasts shivering as they ate up greedily the corn—but for whose eating properties they had died of the cold—the hardships of the Siberian traveller wending his way from the Ural Mountains to Kamchatka.

On this same night, the westbound stage was stuck in a snowdrift somewhere between Fort Harker and Fort Larned. On board were the company messenger and Theodore R. Davis, correspondent for Harper's New Monthly Magazine, *on his way to join General Hancock's expedition. Davis and his companion spent a cold night in the stage, fortified by both canned and bottled corn, with wolves circling and howling outside.*

Isaac says there were three generals waiting to receive the Indian chiefs. There were actually five: Generals Hancock, Smith, Custer, Gibbs, and Inspector General J. W. Davidson.

On the evening of the 12th of April, the storm having subsided, Generals Hancock, Smith and Custer, with their respective officers, assembled around a great log fire about 8 o'clock. Soon after, through the darkness of night, ten or twelve Indians were seen to approach us. Shrouded in buffalo robes and furs, decorated with every ornament that a savage's most fantastic fancy could devise, they presented, under cover of the night, the incarnate image of just so many devils. After the usual salutations of shaking hands and a "How!" uttered loudly and emphatically, the red men seated themselves by the log fire. The first twenty minutes were occupied with a smoke. The pipe of peace was passed all around; everyone had to take a puff. From time immemorial, the calumet has figured in Indian history as the god of peace and war, the arbiter of life and death, though there is less superstitious reverence attached to it now than there was formerly done.

Now the smoke would pour in great streams from the nostrils and now ascend upwards, from the mouth as a propitiatory offering to the genii, who dwell in the sky. Among the great chiefs present, Tall Bull and White Horse were the spokesmen for this council.[2] The following "talk" between General Hancock and Tall Bull will not only be interesting in itself, but will give the reason for, and the object of, the Campaign. Edmund Guerrier, a half-Cheyenne interpreter and guide, translated, sentence by sentence, as General Hancock spoke, which was as follows:[3]

"I told your Agent some time ago that I was coming here to see you, and if any of you wanted to speak to me, you could do so. Your agent is your friend. I don't find many chiefs here; what is the reason? I have a great deal to say to the Indians, but I want to talk with them altogether. I want to say it at once, but I am glad to see what chiefs are here. Tomorrow I am going to your camp. I have a boy, said to be a Cheyenne, whom the Cheyennes claim. We have made a promise in which we pledged ourselves, if possible, to find this boy and a girl who were somewhere in the United States. We have found the boy and here he is, ready to be delivered to his nearest relatives, who may call for him. I will leave him at Fort Larned with the commander; he will deliver him up to them. The girl is near Denver. We have written for her, and she will no doubt be sent here, either to your agent, or to the commander of Fort Larned, for delivery to her relatives. You see the boy has not been injured; the girl will be delivered by us also uninjured. Look out that any captives in your hands be restored to us equally uninjured. I tell you these things now, that you may keep your treaties.

"Now I have a great many soldiers, more than all the tribes put together. The Great Father has heard that some Indians have taken white men and women captives. He has heard also that a great many Indians are trying to get up war to try to hunt the white men. That is the reason I came down here. I intend, not only to visit you here, but my troops will remain among you, to see that the peace and safety of the Plains is preserved. I am going, also, to visit you in your camp. The innocent, and those that are truly our friends, we shall treat as brothers. If we find, hereafter, that any of you have lied to us, we will strike them. In case of war, we shall punish whoever befriends our enemies. If there are any tribes among you who have captives, white or black, you must give them up safe and unharmed as they are now. I have collected all the evidence of all the outrages committed by you, so that your agent may examine into the matter and tell me who are guilty and who are innocent. When your agent informs me who the guilty are, I will punish them. When just demands are made, I will enforce them if they be not acceded to. I have heard that a great many Indians want to fight. Very well; we are here, and we come prepared for war. If you are for peace, you know the conditions; if you are for war, look out for its consequences. If we make war, it will be made against the tribe, who must be responsible for the acts of their young men. Your agent is your friend, but he knows his friendship will not save you from the anger of your Great Father, if we go to war. If we find any good Indians, and they come to us with clean hands, we will treat them as brothers, and we will separate them from the malcontents, and provide for them if necessary. This we will do that the innocent may escape the war which will be waged against the guilty. The soldiers are going to stay in the country, and they will see that the white man keeps his treaty as well as the red man. We are building railroads and building roads through the country. You must not let your young men stop them; you must keep your young men off the roads. These roads will benefit the Indians as well as the white man in bringing their goods to them cheaply and promptly. The steam-car and wagon train must run, and it is of importance to the whites and Indians that the mails, goods and passengers carried on them shall be safe. You know very well, if you go to war with the white man, you would lose. The Great Father has plenty more warriors. It is true you might kill some soldiers and surprise some small detachments, but you would lose men, and you know that you have not a great many to lose. You cannot replace warriors lost; we can. It is to your interest, therefore, to have peace with the white man.

"Every tribe ought to have a great chief; one that can command his men. For any depredations committed by any one of his tribe, I shall hold the chief and his tribe responsible. Some Indians go down to Texas and kill women and children.[4] I shall strike the tribes they belong to. If there are any good Indians, who don't want to go to war, I shall protect them. If there are any bad chiefs, I will help the good chiefs to put their heels on them. I have a great many chiefs with me that have commanded more men than you ever saw, and they have fought more great battles than you have fought fights. A great many Indians think they are better armed than they were formerly, but they must recollect that we are also. My chiefs cannot derive any distinction from fighting with your small numbers; they are not anxious for war against Indians, but are ready for a just war, and know how to fight and lead their men. Let the guilty, then, beware, I say to you, to show you the importance of keeping treaties made with us, and of letting the white man travel unmolested. Your Great Father is your friend as well as the friend of the white man. If a white man behaves badly, or does wrong to you, he shall be punished if the evidence ascertained at the trial proves him guilty. We can redress your wrongs better than you can.

"I have no more to say. I will await the end of this council to see whether you want war or peace. I will put what I say in black and white, and send it to each post commander in the country I command; you can have it read to you when you please, and you can come back after a while and read it, and you will know whether we have lied to you or not."

This speech was received by the Indians with a "Ugh!" and this same guttural exclamation was indulged in from time to time during the speech, when the general would utter something that pleased or displeased them. The Indian brain was now soothed by another smoke, the pipe being passed all around; when Tall Bull, a tall, slender wiry looking Indian who reminded me very much of Shakespeare's Cassius, having "a lean and hungry look," stepped out, and spoke as follows:

"You sent for us, we came here. We have made the treaty with our agent, Colonel Wynkoop.[5] We never did the white man any harm. We don't intend to. Our agent told us to meet you here. Whenever you want to go on the Smoky Hill, you can go; you can go on any road. When we come on the road, your young men must not shoot us. We are willing to be friends with the white man. This boy you have here, we have seen him; we don't recognize him. He must belong to some tribe south of the Arkansas. The buffalo are diminishing fast. The antelope, that were plenty a few years ago, they are now thin. When they shall all die away, we shall be hungry; we shall want something to eat and will be compelled to come into the fort. Your young men must not fire on us. When they see us, they fire, and we fire on them.

"The Kiowas, Comanches, Apaches and Arapahoes, send and get them here and talk with them. You say you are going to the village tomorrow. If you go, I shall have no more to say to you there than here. I have said all I want to say here. I don't know whether the Sioux are coming or not; they did not tell me they were coming. I have spoken."

At the conclusion of Tall Bull's speech, each Indian uttered the usual "Ugh!" The warrior, folding his robes around him, sat down by the log fire and all indulged in a smoke—the pipe of peace being passed around again.

The Indian warrior spoke like one who, feeling his weakness, was yet not afraid to speak the feelings of his heart at all hazards. After a few minutes General Hancock replied as follows:

"I did not come here to see you alone; I came to see the Arapahoes, Comanches, Kiowas and Apaches, when I learn where they are. I was told that some Indians were seeking for war. I want to see those who are friendly and those who are not and wish for war. You say that the soldiers and other white people fire on you when you go to the Smoky Hill. That was because your young men went there to molest the white people, and fired on them first. We know the buffalo are going away, but we cannot help it. The white men are becoming a great nation. You must keep your young men off the roads. Don't stop trains and travellers on the roads, and you will not be harmed. You ought to be friends to the white man.

Soldiers expect to be killed when they are at war. Their business is to fight, but as fast as our soldiers are killed we can get more to take their places. But you must keep off the great roads across the Plains, for if you should ever stop one of our rail-road trains, and kill the people in it, you would be exterminated. You must go to the white man to be taken care of hereafter, and you should cultivate his friendship. That is all I have to say."

This was my first experience in Indian councils; and I have recorded it in full, because the knowledge of such proceedings—even in this age of diplomacy—is very infrequent, because it partially explains the causes of the war, and again to discover to the world how tyrannical, dictatorial and insolent this government is over Indians. It is the same old story of might makes right. Now the Indian is a man in every sense of the word; and like most other men, he has his share of reason, pride and ambition. And how galling it must have been to those Indian warriors—whose fearless hearts had braved a thousand dangers—to be talked to as if they were children. The "musts" and "wills" and "shalls" were more wounding to them than steel-pointed arrows. General Hancock talked to those Indian warriors and orators as a cross schoolmaster would to his refractory scholars. I do not find fault, in saying this, with the General. He is a soldier, and a soldier's tongue is not given to soft phrases, and then he was sent on the Plains to intimidate and, if necessary, make war on the Indians.

General Hancock's speech sounded arrogant and patronizing to Isaac Coates, who regarded the Indian chiefs as leaders of independent nations. Isaac was indignant that Hancock would address them as recalcitrant children, but the army had looked on Indians as insurgents rebelling against a sovereign nation since 1849, when the War Department turned the Indian problem over to the Department of the Interior. Part of Isaac's resentment probably came from his perception that the Indians knew as well as he how absurd it was to declare that the new roads would benefit them as well as the white man and that the white man could "redress" the Indians' wrongs better than they could. If the Indians had learned anything in twenty years of increasing contact with the white man, it was that the white man never redressed Indian wrongs and, whenever possible, actually made them worse. Hancock's demand that every tribe should have one commander-in-chief would have seemed equally ridiculous to Isaac. He understood that such an arrangement would be convenient for the army because one Indian could then be held responsible for problems. But he also knew, as Hancock should have, that Plains Indians lived in loosely organized societies that broke up for the winter into bands or families and only came together in larger groups for the spring and summer hunting. In the last ten years of their free-ranging existence, long after the campaign of 1867, the tribes did begin to create and rely on powerful war chiefs like Red Cloud, but that change came about only when their culture was profoundly threatened.

Historians are divided about the consequences of Hancock's conference with the Indians on the night of April 12, which is not suprising when one considers how widely the accounts of the witnesses diverge. Henry M. Stanley is often quoted as the authoritative record of the discussion, but Stanley does not even mention, as Isaac does, that Hancock made two separate statements, the second of which was more accusatory and bellicose than the first. After reporting the first half of Hancock's speech and Tall Bull's response, Stanley comments on Indian atrocities and a justification for the military expedition. Custer, who also listened to the exchange, says only that Hancock explained to the Indians why he had come, what he expected of them, and that he was not there to make war but to promote peace. Custer dismisses Tall Bull's address, which affected Isaac so profoundly, as containing nothing important. Theodore R. Davis, on the other hand, does report that Hancock spoke again, asking why more chiefs were not present and insisting that he was going to move his force closer to the Indian village whether the Indians liked it or not.

Up to this point in the campaign, everything had gone more or less according to the plan that generals Sherman and Hancock had worked out early in March. With the council of April 12, however, Hancock entered a new world. Suddenly he was negotiating face-to-face with people of a different culture, different traditions, and different religious beliefs. His former adversaries—Confederate generals—had often been fellow graduates of West Point. Indian leaders did not follow the same rules. The April 12 meeting was the first in a series of events and decisions that would produce intense criticism of Hancock's leadership, immediately following the end of the expedition and persisting until this day.

Without question, Hancock made serious errors in the conduct of the campaign from that moment on, but it has never been clear why those mistakes were made. Part of the problem, it seems, is that the few primary sources available to scholars are, as has been previously noted, uneven in their accuracy and objectivity. Stanley, for example, one of the most frequently quoted eyewitnesses, wrote vivid, detailed descriptions of the people and places he saw on the march but had his own biases that affected his accounts of the most controversial incidents. For instance, he was so convinced that the "red fiends," the Sioux and Cheyennes, were conspiring "for evil purposes" that he describes the delay of Hancock's council with the chiefs as follows: "He had waited patiently at Larned for the chiefs to come to the council, but they only came in groups of twos and threes five days after the day appointed for it, which involved him in endless embarrassment."[6] Stanley does not mention the snow storm that all of the other witnesses agree was one of the main reasons for the delay.

Hancock is criticized, by George Grinnell among others, for holding the meeting at night and thereby creating suspicion among the chiefs, because friendly meetings were customarily held in the daytime. In My life on the Plains, *Custer says that the Cheyenne Dog Soldier chiefs visited the camp in the evening and "expressed a desire to hold a conference." Davis, on the other hand, gives quite a different picture in his article in* Harper's New Monthly Magazine, *saying that the Indians arrived late in the afternoon, asked for and received food, and retired to a Sibley tent provided for them. He also says that several officers were ordered to dress in their loudest uniforms, a large fire was built, and the Indians emerged from their tent to begin the council "two hours after dark." Isaac Coates describes the dramatic appearance of the chiefs in the firelight but does not comment on how the meeting came about. We do not know who was to blame for holding the meeting at night or if it did indeed cause mistrust. There is no record of Hancock being advised by the Indian agents or General Smith to defer the meeting until the following morning.*

FOUR

The March up the North Fork of the Pawnee

THE COUNCIL HAD revealed the fact that the Indian village composed of Sioux and Cheyennes, numbering 500 to 600, was on Pawnee Fork, about 35 miles from Fort Larned. General Hancock determined to march to the village. Colonel Wynkoop, the Indian agent, protested against this, declaring that the Indians would be intimidated by the troops, and would run away, fearing another Sand Creek massacre (which will be described hereafter). But General Hancock came to intimidate the Indians (not knowing, Alas! that to intimidate them was rather to point their arrows with steel than to unstring their bows). So, on the morning of the 13th of April, the command moved up Pawnee Fork. Having some difficulty in crosssing it, and being compelled to build a bridge for that purpose, we marched but 21 or 22 miles that day. During the day Indians were to be seen all over the country, moving in the direction of the village. Some were mounted and others were afoot. They came up close to the column and exchanged a "how" with us. Now and then, a squaw and two or three papooses would be seen on a poor miserable pony that would swagger under its load like a drunken man.

The Indians had set fire to the grass, which was burning and smoking all over the country, thinking to interfere with our approach to their village. This is part of their stratagem in war; and would have answered admirably had we had no hay or corn for the horses and team mules.

During the early part of the afternoon Pawnee Killer, a chief of the Sioux, accompanied by four or five Sioux and Cheyenne warriors, came up with us and rode along conversing with General Hancock.[1] White Horse, a Cheyenne chief, with several warriors, came up about the same time and engaged in conversation with General Hancock through the interpreter. Most of these by invitation of the General, remained in the camp during the night and were to hasten the chiefs in early next morning. The excessively cold weather, which had up to this time torpidised me into mental and physical inertia, had now been exchanged for a bright, warm sun, a milder atmosphere, and a spring-like aspect of nature. I was just now beginning to awaken to the novelties and interest of the expedition.

Early on the next morning (Sunday, 14th of April), Pawnee Killer left our camp to hurry in the chiefs who were to be present at 9 A.M., which the Indians expressed by pointing to that part of the heavens which was mid-way between the horizon and the zenith. The hour arrived and no Indians came. The General forgot (or did not care to recollect) that savages, counting their time by "moons" or "sleeps," were not accustomed to "keep time like a watch," to be "punctual as lovers to the moment sworn"; that they were strangers to the momentary exactment of appointments, like the white man, as they are strangers to the speed of the locomotive and the lightning of the telegraph. At 9:30 A.M., Bull Bear, a Cheyenne chief, came in and reported that the chiefs were on their way and would soon arrive.[2] This want of punctuality on the part of the poor savages, the General treated with as much rigor as if the Indians had been white soldiers. The time had passed for the council at this camp and he would defer it until the next one, that evening, near their village. Bull Bear assented to this; and we broke camp and marched up the stream at 11:00 A.M. We had gone but a few miles, when reaching the summit of a little hill, we beheld in the valley, a mile distant, several hundred Indian warriors approaching us. They were in a line and presented to us a splendid appearance. Everything now looked like war; an engagement was momentarily expected, and it was even reported at the rear that hostilities had commenced. We expected, like Leonidas at Thermopoli, to see arrows darken the heavens.[3]

Our column was halted at once, the infantry and artillery formed in a line, and the cavalry came galloping up to the front with drawn sabers. The whole command, together with the pontoon train and the wagon train, had as formidable appearance and as warlike an aspect as anything of the kind during the late war. After approaching within a few hundred yards, the Indians halted, became unsteady, and those who were not mounted, fled. The mounted warriors were not still for one moment. Every horse was in motion. This is a peculiar feature in Indian warfare which compels the enemy to shoot on the wing as it were. The 300 warriors moving to and fro in this manner presented a spectacle as if a myriad persons were treading the mazy dance—it was unique.

In a letter to Libbie, General Custer said that many of his officers pronounced the array of Indian warriors facing them to be the most beautiful sight they had ever seen. Stanley makes the curious statement that there were "no signs of hostility on our part."

Having permission of General Hancock, Colonel Wynkoop rode forward into the Indian lines and reassured them with his presence that no harm was imminent. It was plain to be seen how overjoyed they were to see their agent. Colonel Wynkoop, with Roman Nose (who bore a white flag), Bull Bear, White Horse, Grey Beard, and Medicine Wolf, Cheyenne Chiefs; and Pawnee Killer, Little Bear, and The Bear That Walks Under The Ground, Sioux Chiefs, rode forward and were met by Generals Hancock, Smith and Custer together with several of their officers.

The wind was cold and blowing strongly at the time, and the General did not feel disposed to waste much time with the red warriors. Accordingly, he asked them at once if they were anxious to fight—saying that he was ready. They replied in the negative, declared their friendship, and said they did not desire war and did not wish to fight. He then informed them that he would camp close by their village that night and would hold a council with them as soon as his tent was pitched. A few of the chiefs remained with us, the rest going back to their warriors, who at once faced

about and started for their village. The Sioux, who were mostly dismounted, had started back some time before the others.

Of all the chiefs, Roman Nose attracted the most attention. He is one
of the finest specimens, physically, of his race. He is quite six feet in
height, finely formed with large body and muscular limbs. His appearance
decidedly military, and on this occasion, particularily so, since he wore the
full uniform of a General in the Army. A seven-shooting Spencer carbine
hung at the side of his saddle, four large Navy revolvers stuck in his belt,
and a bow, already strung, with a dozen or more arrows, were grasped in
his left hand. Thus armed, and mounted on a fine horse, he was a good
representative of the God of War; and his manner showed plainly that he
did not care much whether we talked or fought.[4]

*When General Hancock rode forward from the line of troops, he could have been
riding to his death. Grinnell says that Roman Nose had just told Bull Bear that
he intended to shoot Hancock when they came close to each other. Bull Bear begged
Roman Nose not to do it for the sake of the women and children in the village.*

*Although Wynkoop's intercession was important, and although he took the
greatest risk in moving alone into the Indian line of battle, Hancock does not
mention Wynkoop in his official report: "I halted the troops and directed the Indians to halt also. I then invited the chiefs to an interview, and rode forward to
meet them between the lines, accompanied by General Smith, General Custer,
and a few other officers." Custer, Stanley, and Davis also failed to report Wynkoop's role in reassuring the chiefs that Hancock did not intend to attack the village.*

*On April 14, Hancock had written General Sherman that he had "appointed
9 o'clock for the interview" with the Indians, that Pawnee Killer had said early
that morning that the chiefs "would hardly be in before 10 or 11," and that Bull
Bear had arrived at 9:30 and reported, as Isaac Coates says he did, that the
chiefs were on their way and would soon arrive. Hancock, therefore, had reasonable assurance that the chiefs intended to meet with him that morning. Nevertheless, he decided not to wait and set out for the village at 11:00 A.M. Custer
wrote later that Bull Bear was indulging in "mere artifice to secure delay," but*

this seems unlikely. Wynkoop wrote to his superior that the Indian village was at least ten miles farther from the army camp than had at first been supposed and that the chiefs had started out to meet with Hancock as soon as they received his message. Davis says that Hancock waited for the Indians until noon before packing up and leaving, a statement that would justify Hancock's impatience if it were true. The Indians may have been tardy because they could not ride the extra ten miles quickly enough on their emaciated horses. In any case, they rode the distance in vain. Hancock did not wait.

In describing the line of Indian warriors confronting him on the way to the village, Hancock says he was surprised because "it was not part of the programme." Hancock was to find that nothing would go according to plan for the next several weeks, as he floundered from one unanticipated predicament to another. Just why he was so obsessed with forcing the Indian women and children to return to the village remains a mystery. Perhaps his ego was damaged by their flight, since it implied a lack of confidence in his intentions or perhaps he simply interpreted any action that did not fit the "programme" as a hostile act. Ironically, the more emphatic Hancock became, the more the Indians were convinced that he did indeed intend to massacre the women and children.

After writing in his April 14 report to Sherman that he had been told the women and children were fearful of another Chivington massacre, Hancock expressed his doubts about the Sioux chiefs: "If they do not return I shall feel inclined to think they have been doing something wrong." And later the same night, after midnight, Hancock added to his report that Edmund Guerrier, the interpreter, had returned from the village with the news that the warriors had also fled. In their flight, they had cut pieces of material from their lodges. Isaac Coates and other witnesses, including Davis, recognized that those fragments had been cut to protect, as Isaac put it, the "homeless, half-clad fleeing savages ... lying on the frost-carpeted earth and facing the cold April wind, half-naked." Hancock, however, believed Fall Leaf, his Delaware Indian guide, who told him that cutting the lodges was a hostile act. He reported to Sherman: "This looks like commencement of war." Later, on May 22, Hancock wrote that the Indians had abandoned their village because "they felt guilty on account of past offences and intended to make war."

A half hour elapsed, the Indians were out of sight and the column moved on. Bull Bear, who, with some of the other chiefs remained with us, beseeched General Hancock not to go to the Indian village, for the reason that his formidable military array would frighten their women and children, and cause them to run away—apprehending another horrible Sand Creek massacre—but the General's mind was made up. Not intending any harm to them, he did not pause to consider their just grounds for fear, and moved on, camping that afternoon within a few hundred yards of their village, after a march of 10 miles, and something over thirty from Fort Larned.

The Indian village was situated in a beautiful grove on the North Fork of Pawnee Creek, a most charming spot; the buffalo grass, which was just beginning to grow, was soft as velvet to the feet. In this lovely abode the red man had been living, remote from the public highway, in peace and quietness. But now the army, like a destructive earthquake, had come to demolish their habitations, and send them fleeing, homeless, for their lives. Guards were stationed around our camp to prevent the soldiers from going to the village. A few poor Indian ponies grazing near us were sent to the Indians. Soon after our encampment, General Hancock summoned the principal chiefs, and Roman Nose, Medicine Wolf, Bull Bear and Grey Beard, Cheyennes, were not long in answering the summons. They informed the General that the women and children were so terrified on seeing the troops approach, and fearing that they would all be massacred as the Indians were at Sand Creek, ran off leaving everything behind them, and that the Sioux, too, who were mostly dismounted, had fled with them.

In the course of the "talk," Roman Nose showed his bold and fearless spirit. When General Hancock enquired, somewhat decidedly, why the women and children had fled on his approach; the Indian asked him whether the women and children of the whites were not afraid of anything; that he and his comrades were men and warriors, and were not afraid of General Hancock and his troops, but that the women and children were afraid, and had run away. Roman Nose also asked the General if he had not heard of the butchery of Indians at Sand Creek, by U.S.

troops under Colonel Chivington, when the troops came much in the same manner as his troops had approached their village.

The General looked on their abscondence as an act of treachery, and demanded that the chiefs should return them. This two or three of them agreed to attempt to do though they were doubtful as to their success.

FIVE

The Indian Village

THE INDIANS BORROWED two horses of General Hancock, and set out early in the evening after their people that had fled. In the meantime, Guerrier, a half-breed Cheyenne interpreter, was sent to the village with instructions to report every two hours any movement the Indians might make. At 9:30 P.M., those who borrowed the horses having returned them, stated they could not induce their people to return. He reported that the warriors were saddling up, and gathering together whatever they could carry preparatory to leaving the village. Except the sentinels on guard, the camp was in slumbers; for the day's march, though short, was fatiguing; and I was not among the wakeful sleepers. But the news of the Indians departing was carried by whispers from tent to tent. "Let no man speak a loud word," was the order, while the cavalry was ordered to prepare immediately to march. The midnight fairies driving their cars over the dewy lawn of moonlight night in May would not have done it more noiselessly than the 7th Cavalry saddled and mounted their war steeds. The proceeding was a profound mystery. Some declared a myriad Indians were about to attack us; others that we were going to surround the village and massacre the Indians. The night was breathless and beautifully moon-lit. It was more fit for the whispering of lovers' vows than for the terrible voice of Mars. In obedience to General Custer's orders I took my place on his right, with orders to keep there, which had the effect of changing the current of my thoughts, somewhat, from conjectures about our movements to a mathematical certainty that whatever transpired, I should, at least, have the fullest benefit of; for Custer's reputation for fighting was alike high for brilliancy and fearlessness; and if any risks were taken, those near the General would have their full share.

Just why Custer ordered Isaac Coates to stay at his right side and why he chose Isaac, whose only military training was as a navy surgeon, to be one of the four participants in a highly dangerous mission is not clear. The most likely explanation is that he enjoyed Isaac's company and wanted him to share in the excitement. Custer, whose own courage, if not judgment, was beyond question, knew a brave man when he saw one.

Finally, about ten o'clock, the command moved off almost as noiselessly as the big round moon climbed the black hill of night, leaving the infantry and artillery parading under arms. In a few minutes, we reached the Indian village; a deep ravine—forming a natural moat—completely encompassed it; we paused at the brink of this for some minutes; no sound could be heard in the village; the city of wigwams was plainly visible in the bright moonlight, but no dog barked and no human voice or footsteps could be heard; the General urged his horse down the side of the precipitous bank and then up the other, I following; in five minutes the whole command was circling round the village, which had been deserted. Dismounting, we went from lodge to lodge looking for Indians, examining the numerous curious articles which each contained; it was evident that the majority of the furniture had been carried away; though the quantity and variety that remained will astonish the reader when, in a future chapter, the inventory of the village shall be given.

For some reason, perhaps modesty, Isaac Coates confines his description of the moments just before the troopers entered the village to a few sentences. General Custer, on the other hand, writes with glee about the excitement and mystery of not knowing if the Indians were in the village waiting for them. "I dismounted, and taking with me Guerrier, the half-breed, Dr. Coates, one of our medical staff, and Lieutenant Moylan, the adjutant, proceeded on our hands and knees toward the village." Guerrier, whose Cheyenne wife lived in the village, called out several times in Cheyenne but the only reply was the barking of "a score or more of Indians dogs." The presence of so many dogs convinced Guerrier that the Indians were there waiting to pounce. After a brief conference, it was decided the small party should find out whether the village was occupied or not, without calling for reinforcements. "Forward was the verdict. Each one grasped his revolver, resolved to do his best, whether it was running or fighting. I think most of us would have preferred to take our own chances at running. ... The doctor, who was a great wag, even in moments of greatest danger, could not restrain his propensities in this direction. When everything before us was being weighed and discussed in the most serious manner, he remarked: 'General, this recalls to my mind those beautiful lines:

Backward, turn backward, O Time, in thy flight,
Make me a child again just for one night—[1]
This night of all others.'[2]

Going into a chief's lodge with the Indian interpreter, Guerrier, we found a large iron pot suspended over a heap of live coals. The odor issuing from the pot was quite savory, and an examination of its contents showed it to contain dog soup. This was a "dish for the gods" according to Guerrier's palate; and he set to work at once helping himself, now and then pausing to eulogize the delicious beverage and to urge me to join him. Like a good Epicure, wishing to be ignorant of no dish, I joined the half-breed, and for a few minutes, did Indian justice to the stewed canine. It was highly seasoned, decidedly palatable, and taking it all in, I suppose "I ne'er shall look upon its like again." I found nothing whatever disgusting about this great Indian dish, as might be supposed. Now, I would take the meat from a bone, and now a large spoonful of the soup. Though while bearing, thus truthfully, my testimony as to its edible qualities, I do not know that I should take permanent boarding where dog-soup was served daily.

Custer described the event somewhat differently, perhaps embellishing it a little: "The doctor, ever on the alert to discover additional items of knowledge, whether pertaining to history or science, snuffed the savory odors which arose from the dark recesses of the mysterious kettle. Casting about the lodge for some instrument to aid him in his pursuit of knowledge, he found a horn spoon, with which he began his investigation of the contents, finally succeeding in getting possession of a fragment which might have been the half of a duck or rabbit judging merely from its size. 'Ah' said the doctor, in his most complacent manner, 'here is the opportunity I have long been waiting for. I have often desired to test and taste of the Indian mode of cooking. What do you suppose this is?' holding up a dripping morsel. Unable to obtain the desired information, the Doctor, whose naturally good appetite had been sensibly sharpened by his recent exercise a la quadruped, set to with a will and ate heartily of the mysterious contents of the kettle. 'What can this be?' again inquired the doctor. He was only satisfied on one point, that it was delicious—a dish fit for a king.

Just then, Guerrier, the half-breed entered the lodge. He could solve the mystery, having spent years among the Indians. To him the doctor appealed for information. Fishing out a huge piece, and attacking it with the voracity of a hungry wolf, he was not long in determining what the doctor had supped so heartily upon. His first words settled the mystery: 'Why, this is dog.' I will not attempt to repeat the few but emphatic words uttered by the heartily disgusted member of the medical fraternity as he rushed from the lodge."[3]

Entering another lodge, we found an old, crippled, sick Sioux who, being unable to travel, was abandoned by his tribe. But this was military necessity, and no more cruel than military necessities are in civilized armies where, on the field of battle, or in hasty retreat, the wounded are often abandoned, and the dying left with the dead.

"With his lighted faggot in one hand and cocked revolver in the other, the doctor cautiously entered the lodge."[4]

Visiting another lodge, we heard a suppressed moaning. When a buffalo robe from which the sound issued was removed, a little Indian girl 8 or 10 years of age, was discovered. She was a most pitiable spectacle: perfectly naked, eyes mattering and swollen, hair matted and tangled into knots; and blood trickling down her legs. By order of General A. J. Smith, I made an examination of this child and an official report of her condition. Her person had been brutally outraged; and here she was, abandoned and alone, and suffering all the terrible consequences. She was immediately taken care of, and afterwards sent to Fort Dodge. What became of her subsequently, I never learned. At first it was supposed that the Indians had committed the outrage, which called down vengeance on their village from General Hancock. The girl was at first supposed to be white, or at least half-breed, and that on this account the Indians had committed the cruel deed. But subsequent investigation showed the child to be an Indian—and it was then a question whether our own troops, and not the Indians, had not been guilty of the outrages. Colonel Wynkoop, who declared the girl was an Indian (and an idiot), said that there was no instance on record of Indians committing such an outrage on one of their own people.

There were several Indian ponies found in the village, too poor and weak to be taken away. Two of these had so little strength left that, coming up against them with the momentum gained in two or three steps, I pushed them over on the ground. These poor little brutes subsist during the winter entirely on the bark and twigs of the cottonwood tree, a species of poplar. And not withstanding their emaciated, almost starved and dead—and—alive condition in the early spring, so soon as the buffalo grass comes, they fatten like moles and in a few days even, regain their strength and high spirits. In some of the ponies that were left, I observed a small round hole leading between the ribs into the cavity of the chest; and during each expiration and inspiration, the wind would make a low whistling sound, as it passed in and out—perhaps a worm had been the surgeon, who without knife or blood, had performed the operation of parenciutesis thoracis.

The Sioux and Cheyenne lodges, numbering about 300, stood close together, and by the moonlight were not distinguishable one from another. Some of the lodges had large pieces cut out of them, evidently to provide shelter for those who had left them behind, and were now houseless.

This midnight wandering by moonlight through the grass paved streets and tenantless houses of the nomadic city, was less romantic and classical than wending one's way at the same hour o'er the crumbling walls of the Coliseum, or stumbling among the broken columns of Palmyra, but there was a wild and strange novelty in it that to me was intensely fascinating.

We left the Indian village, after securing many curious articles, and returned to camp about midnight; and thus ended Sunday, the 14th of April, 1867—to me the most checkered and eventful Sabbath within the history of my recollection.

Everyone who heard about the discovery of the injured, frightened little girl was outraged by such cruelty, and predictably, most of the whites immediately blamed the Indians. General Hancock, employing a combination of poetic license and bad logic, reported that he, "upon a personal examination," found the girl himself, determined that she had been attacked by Indians, and decided on the spot to burn the Indian village, adding that he would wait to hear from Custer, who was out chasing Indians, before doing so. Fall Leaf, his Delaware advisor, told him that the girl had "white blood." Custer remembered the child's voice as "unmistakably Indian." Davis said the child had suffered "a most abominable outrage" from the Indians. Stanley wrote, with characteristic enthusiasm, that the little girl "according to the surgeon, has been outraged by no less than six Indians." The surgeon, of course, was Isaac Coates, who had a different view of the entire episode and was unlikely to have said anything of the kind.

SIX

War Between the Arkansas and the Platte

General Custer's orders were to pursue the fleeing Indians as rapidly as possible by marches of forty or fifty miles a day, if necessary. The weather had turned hot, and water for the men and the horses was scarce in the dry, broken prairie south of the Smoky Hill River. On April 15, after a long, hard day of crossing and recrossing Walnut Creek, the command camped along its banks for a short night's rest. Reveille sounded at 2:00 A.M. the next morning, and the troopers were off for another, even longer day. Isaac Coates says, matter-of-factly, that he was so exhausted after several days of disagreeable marches, which began very early in the morning and lasted until late at night, that he slept in the saddle. He acknowledges that the command was "wornout" but never says whether or not he thought the forced marches were a sound strategy; even though, as the expedition surgeon, he observed firsthand the consequences of pushing the men and horses beyond reasonable limits of endurance.

At 5 o'clock the next morning, General Custer, with four squadrons of the 7th Cavalry, moved in pursuit of the Indians, with orders from General Hancock: that it was now war against the Cheyennes and Sioux between the Arkansas and the Platte. Up to this time, the mission of the troops on the Plains had been to scare the Indians, henceforth, to war upon them. And it is to be seen to what effect. Long before the sun was up, the cavalry had wound its length over the great hills that shut out from our view the Indian village. A martial spirit had taken possession of every soul in the command. Those who had been left behind, had growled at their hard fate; and those, Oh! fortunate warriors, who were on the war path rejoiced greatly. Those useless prefixes, brevets, were to be washed away in the blood of the red man leaving the genuine rank; and every officer from general down to second lieutenant was to launch his barque on the same sanguine flood and sail into a higher rank. Enlisted men looked forward to promotion; cooks imagined their carving knives to be cutlasses, and even surgeons—alas! for the spirit of humanity—thought every knife in the instrument case and scalpel a two-edged sword. The dogs, heretofore content with the flesh of the jackrabbit, now, imbibing the spirit of their masters, thirsted like the beasts of old, in the Flavian amphitheater for the blood of human captives; and carrion-birds followed on our wake, and wolves hung on our rear awaiting the Hecatomb of dead Indians that were to strew the Plains.[1] But, as Nasby would have expressed it—they didn't strew.[2]

Oh! it was a glorious sight to behold our army, splendidly organized and equipped with every comfort and martial invention of modern civilization, like bloodhounds on the track of the slave, in hot pursuit of the homeless, half-clad fleeing savages; warriors but half-armed, and women and children, lying on the frost-carpeted earth and facing the cold April wind, half-naked. Achilles might have envied us our glorious distinction.

Our guides struck the trail within a short distance of the Indian village which we followed without difficulty to Walnut Creek. The banks of this stream were so high and precipitous that we were compelled to follow it up for three miles, before being able to effect a crossing; the Indians had been compelled to do the same, as was evinced by their trail. We were so close upon them at this time, that the fires they had used for cooking breakfast, were still burning. They must have been warned of our near approach by their rear guard; for in their sudden departure, they were compelled to leave a mule and several ponies which were tied to trees, still bearing their packs. In one of the packs was discovered, by one of our

Delaware guides, the wardrobe of Roman Nose, containing many of the ornaments and much of his finery, together with an elegant large red feather which the chief had in his hat at the meeting on Pawnee Fork. This was a great treasure to the Delaware, and, as he declared, would bring him much distinction when he returned to his people; and in a moment it had transpired the other Indian guides with high ambition for like achievement, and away they dashed over the hills and were soon out of sight, in their eager desire to obtain some trophy that might signalize their services while on the war path.

To mislead us, the Indians had crossed and recrossed the stream several times; but we pressed steadily on on the main trail, and had come so close upon them by the middle of the afternoon that the dirt torn up by their dragging lodge poles was quite fresh. Though we saw no Indians, the Delawares, who kept several miles in advance and on the high elevations, reported seeing several parties watching us at some distance from the high eminences.

General Custer now entertained hopes of overtaking the Indians before night; and, to accelerate our progress, left the wagons protected by one squadron and pushed on with the other three.

Leaving the wagons meant that the three pursuing squadrons (six companies) would camp without tents and with minimal provisions.

This piece of strategy was parried on the part of the Indians by splitting up in small parties; and before sundown we had lost the trail entirely—the last signs pointing north toward the Smoky Hill.

The command had now marched 35 miles, halting only to water. The General sent the Delawares five or six miles in advance but they were unable to keep the trail. Accordingly, we went into camp for the night. The day had been a most exciting one. Although most of the men in the command had been in the late war, but very few had been on the war path. Everything was new and strange and wonderful. By the warmth and blaze of our log fires that night, a thousand Indian stories were told and exploits

Isaac Taylor Coates
(author's collection).

Isaac Coates, photographed
in his naval uniform, was a
ship's surgeon for the U.S.
Navy during the Civil War
(author's collection).

Left, George Armstrong Custer, in an engraving made from a Matthew Brady photograph; *right,* Edward Wynkoop, Indian agent for the Cheyennes and Arapahos of the Upper Arkansas *(both photos from the Denver Public Library, Western History Collection).*

Gen. Winfield Scott Hancock, one of the most admired Union generals of the Civil War, has been almost universally criticized for his handling of the March 1867 expedition *(Kansas State Historical Society).*

Left, Satanta, a determined and effective Kiowa war leader, impressed Isaac Coates with his oratory; *right*, Pawnee Killer, one of the greatest war chiefs of the Southern Oglala Sioux *(left, Little Bighorn Battlefield National Monument; right, Nebraska State Historical Society)*.

Left, Roman Nose, of the Southern Cheyenne, inspired Coates to write, "His manner showed plainly he did not care much whether we talked or fought"; *right*, a principal chief of the Arapahos, Little Raven was a leader in forging peaceful relations *(left, Kansas State Historical Society; right, Denver Public Library, Western History Collection)*.

An illustration from *Harper's Weekly* of the abandoned Indian village on the North Fork of the Pawnee River *(Kansas State Historical Society)*.

Cheyenne lodges *(Kansas State Historical Society)*.

A *Harper's Weekly* illustration of soldiers putting the abandoned Indian village to the torch on April 19, 1867, on orders from General Hancock. The flames from the burning village served to fan the flames of conflict between Indians and whites on the southern plains *(Kansas State Historical Society)*.

Custer's scouts Medicine Bill Comstock (left) and Edmund Guerrier are depicted in this illustration copied from the June 24, 1867, edition of *Harper's Weekly (Kansas State Historical Society).*

Fort Harker, photographed by Alexander Gardner in 1867 *(Kansas State Historical Society).*

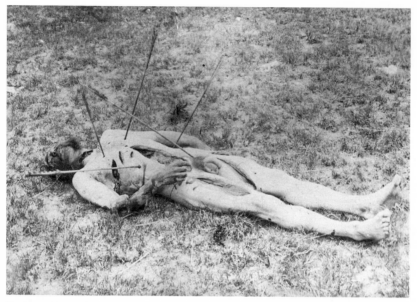

Some victims of Indian attacks were mutilated, which angered (and frightened) soldiers and settlers. Isaac Coates was elsewhere and would not have examined the body of Frederick Wyllyams, sergeant in the Seventh Cavalry, killed June 26, 1867, but he saw other similar corpses—which makes all the more remarkable his sympathy for the Indians' predicament *(Kansas State Historical Society)*.

A *Harper's Weekly* illustration of the June 26, 1867, Indian attack on a wagon train under the command of Lieutenant Robbins. Although greatly outnumbered, the soldiers were able to stay in formation and hold off the Indians for several hours, with minimal losses, until reinforcements arrived *(Kansas State Historical Society)*.

The *Harper's Weekly* for August 3, 1867, included this illustration of mounted soldiers of the Seventh Cavalry under George Custer during the expedition through Kansas and Nebraska *(Kansas State Historical Society)*.

Our guide struck the trail within a short distance of the Indian village, which we followed with difficulty to Walnut Creek. The banks of this stream were so high & precipitous, that we were compelled to follow it up for three miles, before being able to effect a crossing; the Indians had been compelled to do the same, as was evinced by their trail. We were so close upon them at this time, that the fires they had used for cooking breakfast, were still burning. They must have been warned of our near approach by their rear-guard; for in their sudden departure they were compelled to leave a mule, and several ponies which were tied to trees, still bearing their packs. In one of the packs was discovered, by one of our Delaware guides, the wardrobe of Roman Nose, containing many ornaments & much of his finery, together with an elegant large red feather, which the chief had in his hat at the meeting on Pawnee Fork. This was a great treasure to the Delaware, and, as he declared, would bring him much distinction, when he returned to his people; and in a moment it had inspired the other Indian guides with high ambition for like achievement, and away they dashed over the hills, and were soon out of sight, in their eager desire to obtain some trophy that might signalize their services while on the war path.

To mislead us, the Indians had crossed & recrossed the stream several times; but we pressed steadily on on the main trail, and had come so close upon them by the middle of the afternoon that the dirt torn up by their dragging lodge poles was quite fresh. Though we saw no Indians, the Delawares, who kept several miles in advance & on the high elevations, reported seeing several parties watching us at some distance, from the high eminences.

General Custer now entertained hopes of overtaking the Indians before night; and, to accelerate our progress, left the wagons protected by one squadron, & pushed on with the other three.

A page from Isaac Coates's journal *(author's collection)*.

of Indian warriors related from days of King Philip, or Powhatan, to the very chiefs of the tribes we were in pursuit of.[3]

We were on the march the next morning before 4 o'clock heading in the direction of a column of smoke, nearly north, and estimated distance of fifteen miles; smoke was seen also on the high hills both to the east and west. Smoke is the great tell-tale on the Plains; and small parties (and all parties in time of war) on this account never make a fire; though this smoke may have been a piece of stratagem—the Indians often make a smoke to attract their enemies in one direction while they are going in the opposite one.

The Delawares believed that we might find the trail, and, perhaps, the Indian camp. The General pushed on rapidly, following the course of the stream, but before noon, it was discovered that we were beyond the source of the creek, and it would be necessary to retrace our steps for water. We had seen no Indians and no signs of any. The command was now (as we learned afterward) but fifteen miles due south of the Smoky Hill. Had the guides known this—as they should have—we could have marched directly on; but as it was, we had to return nine miles before coming to water. This was not the only instance in which the guides showed their gross ignorance of the Plains. They misled General Hancock in his march from the Indian village toward Fort Dodge, compelling him to camp on the Plains for the night, and reach the fort next day. I could mention many instances in which the so-called guides (who were great guessers) showed their complete incompetence for the service for which they were employed.[4]

It was at this point, where we commenced to retrace our steps, that I saw the first buffalo. We had just gained the summit of a hill, and directly ahead of us we beheld what we supposed to be Indians; they appeared to be coming directly toward us. The longed-for opportunity had now arrived. A harvest of laurels was at hand; and with drawn swords a squadron moved forward to meet the enemy. He had disappeared like a ghost. What could this apparition be? Before long we saw the same foe to the right leading in another direction. It was soon discovered that our enemy was a small herd of buffalo, which we had seen through the delusive atmosphere of the Plains; and that they were some distance off. About the same time we saw to the left, on a distant hillside, what appeared as plain as the noonday sun, the Indians on the march. There were the mounted ponies dragging the lodgepoles—nothing was ever plainer to my eyes. Colonel Benteen was ordered to pursue them. In twenty minutes, with foaming steeds, he had overtaken the enemy—which proved to be a herd of elk. The deceptive element in this case, as with the buffalo, was the peculiar condition of the amosphere known as the mirage, of which more particular mention will be made hereafter.

On retracing our steps for water, and before reaching the stream, the command was thrown into the wildest excitement, by seeing several of our mounted officers, who were some distance ahead, riding at a furious gait. Some declared they were being pursued by Indians, and nothing could exceed the interest manifested for their safety, whilst the whole command was ready and anxious to engage in the anticipated fight. A few minutes, however, revealed the true secret of the fleeing horsemen to be buffalo. And here occurred my first buffalo hunt. Putting spurs to my horse I dashed down the hill, leaped a big ravine, and pellmell, away a dozen of us went together after the fleeing buffalo. General Custer was wild with excitement, and yelled as if he was going into a desperate cavalry charge; nor can I plead "not guilty" of a good many high-keyed notes that would have done no injustice to a raving maniac. Everybody was drunk with excitement and rode at a break-neck gait. A carbine shot had broken the foreleg of one of the buffalo. I rode as near the crippled monster as my frightened horse, who was snorting and rearing like a newly captured wild horse, would go; then dashed away for another one that was holding a party of hunters at bay. This buffalo had been mortally wounded; and it was amusing to see the intense eagerness with which each hunter urged his claim of giving the death shot. As the great monster stood gasping for breath, with expanded nostrils streaming with blood, tongue lolling out and eyes looking death and destruction, he was a frightful spectacle. Lieutenant Owen Hale claimed the buffalo as his—there is honor even among hunters—and with one or two well-aimed shots brought his game to earth. Two of the buffalo out of the few that were seen were killed. They were butchered, and the meat hauled in the ambulance to where we found water and camped at 2:00 P.M. We had marched over 40 miles and had an appetite that did full justice to the wild meat which we passed the afternoon in cooking and eating. No cut of roast beef was ever half so delicious to my taste.

During the day, while General Custer was several miles in advance of the column riding alone on a splendid horse he had had during the war, he was in hot pursuit of a buffalo and coming within pistol range, fired directly ahead of him, at which moment, and while at the top of his speed, the horse threw up his head and receiving the contents of the pistol in his brain, fell with a headlong plunge to the ground flinging the General three or four lengths ahead of him. While the buffalo went on his way rejoicing, the General spent no time in lamentations over the lost game or in grief over the dead horse, but obeying that monarch instinct, self-preservation, set out for the command at a gait that would have done no discredit to Weston, the great pedestrian.[5] I know of nothing that will give so much celerity to a man's gait, or enable him to get more speed out of a horse, than a good Indian scare. I've been there.

Custis Lee, the unfortunate horse in the story about Custer's buffalo hunt, actually belonged to Libbie, who after receiving an apologetic letter from her husband describing the circumstances of the horse's demise, responded not very consolingly that she would never be so fond of an animal again. She added that her grief over Custis Lee was, of course, secondary to her concern for her husband's safety. Isaac Coates comments on the affair with some amusement and a little sympathy, but he and everyone else in the command knew that their commanding officer had been out since daylight chasing antelope with his greyhounds. His only companion, the bugler, who was not riding a thoroughbred, had returned to the column when his horse played out, but Custer went galloping off with his dogs in pursuit of the buffalo he saw in the distance. One of the dogs, young Rattler, became lost and was never recovered.

This episode is often cited by historians as a perfect illustration of Custer's boyish enthusiasm getting the best of his common sense—which some observers have felt Custer lacked to a remarkable degree. Custer wrote Libbie that nothing approaches the excitement of a cavalry charge except a buffalo hunt, and he was not one to pass up a chance for excitement—even though his men were traveling through enemy territory, and his injury or death might have endangered their survival. Custer may also have been violating Hancock's orders that hunting was to be done only under specified circumstances and "straggling" was not to be permitted. The troopers who were told to go back over the prairie and recover Custer's saddle must have had their own opinions about the proceedings, especially when they saw Custer mount a borrowed horse and go galloping after another buffalo.

Between seven and eight o'clock we resumed the march heading north for the Smoky Hill. Since their ponies were so poor and weak, it was expected that we should overtake the Indians on that stream, a favorite resort for them. We had found our very early morning and late evening marches disagreeable; but now we were to have a whole night of it. Accordingly, extra preparations for comfort were taken. The April winds were cold and blew high. I threw a blanket over the saddle so as to protect my knees and feet; and wrapped in the well-known blue army overcoat, I found myself quite comfortable. Our course led over hills, through low bottoms, along streams, across gullies and ravines, and for a portion of the time, through a pretty, heavily timbered country. We had the moon, only now and then obscured by a cloud. Since we might come up with the Indians in the night, every carbine was loaded, and many a finger pressed a trigger during that long and tiresome night's ride. The moon—that nocturnal artist—with its inimitable brush, catering to our excited imaginations, transformed the rocks on the hillsides, and the bushes by the gullies, and the trees in the woods, into painted savages ready with a war whoop to pounce on us. These ghostly apparitions, together with every now and then, the unexpected hoot of an owl, barking of a wolf, and racket in the bushes from some wild beast fleeing on our approach, gave us many a start. I was so exhausted from the fatigue of tonight, added to that from the long march of yesterday, that I slept in the saddle; sometimes, over a smooth surface, riding a mile or two before awaking. At 3:30 the next morning, and after a march of 21 miles, we struck the Smoky Hill, 13

miles west of Downer's Station. We were now on the great highway leading from the East to Denver. No signs of Indians being discovered, we
went into camp until late afternoon. About one o'clock we marched along
the stage road east reaching Downer's at 5:00 P.M. where we camped for
the night. This is one of the Overland Stage Company's stations.

We had not heard or seen anything of Indians up to this point, but here
our most greedy appetite for news was fully satiated. The very air was pregnant with rumors of the red savages. During the day before small bands of
Indians, believed to be Sioux, had been crossing the stage road 30 or 40
miles east, going north. They had burned Lookout Station, run off eighteen horses and four mules; had killed and burned three men employed at
the station, and had scalped one of them. Besides this correct and terrible
news, there were a thousand horrible stories afloat. A western stage driver
can give the honest report, in the shortest possible time, the greatest cor-
pulency. The General concluded to rest the wornout command for the
night, and march eastward next morning. I was so interested in the stories
of the station men and stage drivers, who were blockaded here on account
of the Indians, that I did not go to my blankets until midnight.

The history of one of these frontiersmen, would furnish the most wild
and romantic materials for a book. They are a set of rough, hardy, clever,
loquacious fellows; always having on hand a wonderful and most incred-
ible story, of which the relator is the hero. And while they are recounting
their hardships and threadbare escapes among the Indians, they take particular delight in weaving in an account of their love affairs; how a pair of
new corduroys with brass buttons down the outer leg won the heart of a
village lass—whose fond hopes, Alas!, were never destined to be realized—and how a twenty-five-cent ring had captivated an Indian Beauty.
These and like tales they would tell with a self-relishing gusto, and an air
of triumph really refreshing, but to do these indomitable, hardfisted,
warmhearted fellows justice, it cannot be denied that they are among the
most valuable of our pioneers. They are ready whenever called upon. They
brave all dangers, in a wild savage country, infested with still wilder and
more savage men. Day and night, storm and sunshine, winter's cold and

summer's heat alike, find them with gay hearts and smiling faces, pursuing their hard and perilous avocations.

Downer's Station, where Isaac stayed up until midnight listening to the colorful tales of the frontiersmen, was one of some thirty-five stage stops operated by the Butterfield Overland Despatch between Atchison on the Missouri River and Denver. The number of stations varied considerably over the brief existence of the stage line as conditions on the road changed, and new sites were added while old sites were abandoned. Downer's was a "home station," where stage passengers and drivers could obtain meals—almost always of execrable quality. This elaborate, nearly six-hundred-mile chain of freight and stage stations was entirely a private enterprise. Although its route ran across enemy territory, the company received only occasional help from the army, which sometimes provided escort protection for stagecoaches and, when it could, detailed small detachments of troops to a few of the stations. Most of the time, however, freighters and stage drivers were on their own. Their job was to survive a trip across the plains on the Smoky Hill Trail, considered to be the most dangerous of the three main overland routes from the Missouri River to Denver and New Mexico. The Platte River road to the north and the Santa Fe Trail, to the south along the Arkansas River, were long-established, heavily traveled roads, but the Overland Despatch was comparatively new and its route cut through the middle of the Indians' prime buffalo-hunting grounds. The Indians could not allow it to succeed. Before the spring of 1867, and General Hancock's show of force, they had begun a desperate effort to drive the white man off the Smoky Hill. By the middle of April, only about one station in four was still occupied. The men had consolidated into groups large enough to defend themselves, and the Indians had burned the empty stations. Downer's was one of the most frequently attacked stations on the Smoky Hill road. It had good grass and water, but its setting made it difficult to defend. After repeated raids and some casualties, a small fort was built at the station in May 1867, but the site was abandoned the next year.

Both last evening from Walnut Creek Camp, and this evening, General Custer sent dispatches to General Hancock. I remember on both occasions how many heartfelt good wishes for their safety went after the brave couriers as they set out on their dangerous journey. Mounted on fleet horses, the corporal, five men, and the Delaware guide on this evening galloped off with a cheerful devil-me-care "goodby! boys" and were soon out of sight. They had a distance of seventy miles to go to the Indian village, through a country beset with savage Indians, now thirsting for the blood of the white man. As we caught the last glimpse of them winding their way through the hills to the south, we all felt how uncertain it was that we should ever see them again. Many little incidents like this transpired during our campaign which were calculated to awaken the kindlier feelings in cruel breasts, and to touch the silken cords of the heart that had been attuned for the God of War, with the soft zephyrs of human sympathy, more delicious to the soul than the downy orange-perfumed winds of the sunny south, to the senses.

We marched eastward over the stage road next morning at 5:00 A.M. and reached Lookout Station, a distance of 35 miles, at 3:00 P.M. General Custer went into camp here in order to discover, if possible, what Indians had burnt the station and murdered the men.

Here, to the dreariness of the uncivilized desert, was added all the desolation and horror that arson with its lighted torch and murder with its deadly weapons could add. The stationhouse, the immense stable and the haystack, we found reduced to ashes, and lying near the ruins were the bodies of the three murdered men. A party of employees from Big Creek Station, a few miles west, had been here, attempting to pay the last tribute of respect to their murdered friends; but either through fear or the lack of necessary implements, had merely covered them with a few poles. The wolves had feasted on the legs—the bodies and heads being better protected—until the flesh was torn from the bones. The General had them carefully buried near the station; but previously ordered a medical inspection of the bodies. They were so horribly burnt as scarcely to be recognized. The flesh had been burnt to a crisp, the hair singed from the head, and the intestines were bulging from the abdomen. Our Delaware scouts could form no clue as to the tribe who had committed these depredations. There was not a sign left to tell that any Indians had been there save only the smoking ruins and the dead bodies—mute but terribly logical evidence.

Lookout Station was even harder to defend than Downer's. Unlike many of the stations, Lookout did not have tunnels between the buildings. The stables Isaac mentions were distant from the house and separated from it by a ravine. The men killed by Indians on April 15 were probably trapped in the open between the buildings in which they might have found protection. The site is about six miles south of present-day Hays, Kansas.

This was the first deadly work of the savage Indians that we had seen; and it sent a chill of horror through the whole command. Men whose nerves had been unshaken by the spectacle of a battlefield strewn with dead, shuddered at the sight of these victims of Indian wrath who had been brutally murdered, scalped and burnt. We ourselves had sown the wind and this was the first harvest of the whirlwind. Our Christian, civilized soldiers swore vengeance against the untutored savage; and every man was big with brutal and murderous projects to revenge, on the morrow, the death of their pale-faced brothers that they mourned today.

The whole country now swarmed with Indians. Here, where the stage route had been unmolested for two or three years, Indians were now counted by the hundreds and thousands. The day after we left the Indian village (16th April), 800 Indians, reporting themselves to be Sioux, Pawnees and Cheyennes, crossed the stage route at Stormy Hollow Station going north. They were accoutered in martial attire, half-naked, painted, with strung bows, and quivers full of arrows; and seemed disposed to fight. They ran off several mules which had been left outside the stable. One of the mules got away, but was pursued and fired at until killed. Several shots were fired at the station; and several steel-pointed arrows, carrying burning brands, were successfully lodged in the stable roof, but were withdrawn before setting fire to the building. This is their ingenious mode of practicing incendiarism.

Isaac Coates is not correct when he says that the stage route "had been unmolested for two or three years." The year 1866 was fairly quiet along the Smoky Hill, but during the last three months of 1865, Indians raided stagecoaches and stations in what Theodore Davis called "a general attack along the entire line." Soldiers and civilians were killed, including three Overland Despatch employees at Downer's Station.

At a neighboring station, about this time, a party of 75 or 100 Indians halted; but the employees would permit only the chiefs to approach them. Four of these, believed to be Sioux, giving their names as White Clay, Turkey Egg, Bull Knife, and Big Horse, came up and talked for half an hour. As usual with all Indians, they were very hungry. Some of these chiefs had papers signed by officers at Fort Laramie, some months previous, representing them to be "good Indians." It is customary on the Plains for officers to give these passports to Indians who have proven themselves friendly.

We continued to note the signs of Indians all along the road. Guerrier, the half-breed interpreter and guide, believed the Indians were going to the Solomon, a stream 40 miles north where buffalo are plenty. We remained at Lookout Station for the night, and this day was only less interesting than that of the day we entered the Indian village.

In the dispatches that were sent to General Hancock by General Custer on the night of April 17, Custer reported that the Indians had begun their "long promised attacks" and it was expected that all travel would cease on the Smoky Hill road. He said that he had "no doubt but that the depredations committed at Lookout Station were by some of the same Indians who deserted their lodges on Pawnee Fork." The brave couriers, whom Isaac Coates watched as they set out on their seventy-mile journey, rode all night and arrived in Hancock's camp on the Pawnee Fork on the morning of April 18. On April 19, Custer sent another dispatch to Hancock that included a postscript: "Lookout Station was burned and the men massacred on Monday, the 15th, which clears those Indians who were at Pawnee Fork the day of our arrival from the charge of being present at the murder."

SEVEN

Hancock Burns the Indian Village

THE NEXT DAY, April 19th, we marched directly to Fort Hays, a distance of 20 miles. In four days we had marched 154 miles. General Custer expected to replenish his forage here and march at once after the Indians, but what was his surprise to find that there was no forage at this post for him. His supply was now exhausted, and Fort Hays had but a limited supply of its own, which made but one day's supply for General Custer's command. This he took and dealt out as economically as possible. The horses had stood the hard march well—35 miles a day—but they now needed extra, instead of a limited supply of provender. The weather was cold, and the grass not yet fit for pasturage. The animals must not starve. The General dispatched Wild Bill on a wild mule, as fast as an antelope to Fort Harker, 60 to 70 miles distant, for four days forage. Wild Bill, one of our scouts, was a tall, graceful, fine-looking fellow with good features, fair skin and blue eyes and long flowing hair, hanging over his shoulders, most tempting bait for an Indian scalping knife. The ride must be made in the night. Bill set out after dark, armed to the teeth; with a "Good by! Boys! I'll take my breakfast at Harker's."

It has been suggested by at least one historian that "Wild Bill" was the scout Bill Comstock, but it is more likely, from Isaac Coates's description of him, that he was Wild Bill Hickok.[1] Comstock, who also served as a scout on Custer's 1867 campaigns, was usually called "Medicine Bill." He was probably at Fort Wallace during the last two weeks of April.[2]

As usual with army blunders, nobody was to blame for the lack of forage. Hancock blamed it on the Quartermaster. The Quartermaster blamed it on the high creeks and the high creeks blamed it on the clerk of the weather. The Indians, who had beaten us across the Smoky Hill with their poor ponies, might now repose in safety while we awaited food for the cavalry horses. And while we are awaiting the departure of the next expedition, we will return to General Hancock at the Indian village and see what has transpired on the Arkansas.

Since General Custer's departure from the Indian village, General Hancock had remained there impatiently awaiting news of his progress; and all the while smarting under the humiliating idea of being out-witted by the red savages. He had come out there with an army to lecture them on their bad conduct, to tell them what they should and should not do, where they should and should not go; and lo! they had been so insolently inconsiderate of the world-famous Major General, so ill-mannered and disrespectful, as to march off without his leave or license.

The General had declared that the Indian village ought to be burned as a chastisement for their treachery in running away, to say nothing of the violation of the person of the little half-breed (as she was then supposed to be, but turned out to be a full Cheyenne) girl. The brand was ready for its work when the news of the burning of Lookout Station, and the murder of the three men, arrived. Hancock gave the order and 300 Indian wigwams were immediately wrapped in flames, and soon—with all their contents—reduced to ashes. This loss was as great to the Indians who owned the village, as the destruction of Chicago was to its citizens.

The Indians had run away through fear "which was a grievous fault, and grievously had they answered for it."

It will be no less astonishing than interesting and instructive to give an account of the property found in these two Cheyenne and Sioux villages. The inventory was as follows:

Cheyenne camp—132 lodges, 396 buffalo robes, 57 saddles, 120 travoises, 78 headmats, 90 axes, 58 kettles, 125 frying pans, 200 tin cups, 130 wooden bowls, 116 tin pans, 103 whetstones, 44 sacks of paint, 57 sacks of medicine, 63 water kegs, 14 ovens, 117 rubbing horns, 42 coffee mills, 150 rope lariats, 100 chains, 264 parfleches, 70 coffee pots, 50 hoes, 120 fleshing irons, 200 parfleche sacks, 200 horn spoons, 42 crowbars, 400 sacks of feathers, 200 tin plates, 160 brass kettles, 40 hammers, 15 sets lodge poles (uncovered), 17 stew pans, 4 drawing knives, 10 spades, 2 bridles, 93 hatchets, 25 tea kettles, 250 spoons, 157 knives, 4 pickaxes.

Sioux camp—140 lodges, 420 buffalo robes, 226 saddles, 150 travoises, 142 headmats, 142 axes, 138 kettles, 40 frying pans, 190 tin cups, 146 tin pans, 140 whetstones, 70 sacks of paints, 63 water kegs, 6 ovens, 160 rubbing horns, 7 coffee mills, 280 ropes (lariats), 140 chains, 146 parfleches, 50 curry combs, 58 coffee pots, 32 hoes, 25 fleshing irons, 40 horn spoons, 14 crowbars, 54 brass kettles, 11 hammers, 5 sets lodge poles (uncovered), 4 stew pans, 9 drawing knives, 2 spades, 8 bridles, 3 pitchforks, 3 tea kettles, 280 spoons, 4 pickaxes, 1 sword and extra scabbard, 1 bayonet, 1 mail bag, 1 stone mallet, 1 lance.

General Custer gives the following inventory of captured property in the Indian village on the Washita, I.T., after his great fight and signal defeat of the Indians there on November 28, 1868:

875 ponies, horses and mules, 241 saddles of very fine and costly workmanship, 573 buffalo robes, 390 buffalo skins for lodges, 160 untanned robes, 210 axes, 140 hatchets, 35 revolvers, 47 rifles, 535 pounds of powder, 1,050 pounds of lead, 4,000 arrows and arrowheads, 75 spears, 90 bullet moulds, 35 bows and quivers, 12 shields, 300 pounds of bullets, 775 lariats, 940 buckskin saddle bags, 470 blankets, 93 coats, 700 pounds of tobacco. Besides these, there was their whole supply of winter food— dried buffalo meat, meal, flour, and other provisions.

Isaac Coates gives exactly the same inventory as that provided by Wynkoop to the Commissioner of Indian Affairs. Stanley, on the other hand, uses the inventory supplied by Captain G. W. Bradley, chief quartermaster of the expedition. For some inexplicable reason, there are substantial differences in the numbers.

For example, Wynkoop counted 816 buffalo robes, 283 saddles, and 232 axes. Bradley showed 942 robes, 436 saddles, and 191 axes. Stanley asserted that the Indians had suffered a severe loss and would need to kill three thousand buffalo to replace the hides for their "wigwams." Davis commented that he had heard some estimates of the value of the destroyed property that were "ludicrously large" and guessed that the Indians could replace their losses in a single summer. Nevertheless, Stanley's estimate is the one usually used by historians.

Over the years, the events that followed the failed conference with the Indian chiefs—Hancock's attempts to force the Indians to return, the capture of the village, and, finally, the burning of the village—have received widely differing interpretations among historians. Hancock's decisions and the reasons why he made them have been the subjects of intense debate. There is, however, general agreement among scholars of the West that those few days of mid-April 1867, profoundly influenced relations between the government and Indian tribes across the western plains for the rest of 1867 and beyond. Robert Athearn thought that the burning of the village was a pivotal act that launched a new plains war: "Hancock had interviews with a number of Indians but had no apparent success. Then, on April 19, he struck. His men burned one of the Cheyenne villages on the Pawnee River as punishment for, as Sherman put it, 'depredations and murders previously committed.' With that action, a thrill of terror rippled across Kansas. The whites knew that from then on, every stagecoach driver had better clasp tightly to his scalp and lay on with the blacksnake. The Indians would never forget April 19."[3]

Isaac Coates watched and listened, and drew his own conclusions. He is bitter in his denunciation of Hancock's decision to burn the village, suggesting that Hancock felt humiliated by the Indians' leaving without permission and was looking for any excuse to light the fire. He says "the brand was ready" before Custer's dispatches arrived from Lookout Station. Stanley and Davis wrote that news of the burning of the station and the murder of the three men convinced Hancock to burn the village, which he then proceeded to do forthwith. Indeed, that is the most commonly accepted explanation for Hancock's action, but Isaac thought differently. The official record reveals a more erratic course toward that momentous decision and suggests that Hancock had a terrible time making up

*his mind. Isaac Coates was aware of the preliminary exchanges between Han-
cock and others in the expedition before he left with the Seventh Cavalry in
pursuit of the Indians. And he probably knew that Wynkoop had written Hancock a formal letter on April 13 urging him not to destroy the village and warn-
ing that a general war would break out if Hancock carried through with his
threat. Wynkoop later wrote that Hancock's response "verbally" to him was that,
for the present, he would not burn the village. On April 15, however, Hancock
wrote the commanding officer of Fort Larned that he was going to destroy the
village "unless other developments should make it seem unwise to do so." On
April 17, before the news from the Smoky Hill arrived, he wrote Sherman: "The
Sioux and Cheyenne camps being together on the same ground, it would hardly
be practicable, with our information, to destroy one without destroying the
other. The question is really, whether we shall destroy both, or either, and which.
I think we have provocation sufficient to destroy the camp; still we may not
have, and by burning it we will certainly inaugurate a war which might otherwise have been avoided."[4] He added that General Smith was opposed to burning the camp. General Sherman must have wondered at the echoes of Hamlet
coming from the general who, with shells bursting in every direction and men
diving for cover, had ridden up and down the line on Cemetery Ridge, rallying
his forces to hold the Union center and stand against Pickett's charge.*

*On April 17, Hancock issued Special Field Orders no.12, which said, in part,
"As a punishment for the bad faith practiced by the Cheyennes and Sioux who
occupied the village at this place, and as a chastisement for murders and depredations committed since the arrival of the command at this point by the people
of these tribes, the village recently occupied by them, which is now in our hands,
will be entirely destroyed."[5] On May 23, General Hancock received a telegram
from General Grant requesting an explanation for the decision to burn the village. Hancock submitted a written reply on July 31 saying that he was compelled to take action against Indian "treachery." He also wrote a "communication" on the subject to the* Army and Navy Journal, *which was followed
promptly by a long, detailed rejoinder from Agent Wynkoop that pointed out
what he thought were serious discrepancies in Hancock's version of the story.*

EIGHT

Councils with the Kiowa
and Arapahoe Chiefs

GENERAL HANCOCK marched from the ashes of the Indian village directly for Fort Dodge on the morning of the 20th. The day following, the guides misled him—a thing they very often do—so that he did not reach the post until the 22nd. On the following day, General Hancock held a council with several of the chiefs. The Indians' talk is worthy of being recorded. After the General spoke, to the same purpose as his first speech at Larned, The Man That Moves said: "what the big chief [Hancock] says I believe. So will all the chiefs, every word of it. I am an old man, brother of Te-Haw-Son. What this big chief says, listen to, you young men."

Isaac Coates quotes the text of Kiowa Chief Kicking Bird's speech exactly as it is given in Document 240, but Stanley uses different phrases in several places and omits six sentences. Moreover, throughout his quotation, he uses the name "Kicking Eagle" rather than "Kicking Bird," presumably a variation in the translation of the Kiowa language. It is reasonable to assume that there were several interpreters taking down the words as they were spoken, and Stanley happened to have used a different interpreter than the one used in the official record.

Stanley provides about a third of Hancock's speech, again using many different words and phrases than the transcript reported in Document 240 but giving the same general thrust. The greater part of Hancock's address was devoted to a meticulous accounting of the events of the past ten days, apparently to persuade the Kiowas that the Sioux and Cheyennes had behaved badly and warn them not to make the same mistakes. Hancock said that he wanted "all friendly Indians" to stay south of the Arkansas so the soldiers would not confuse them with the Sioux and Cheyennes, in which case they might be shot. He closed with an invitation to all Kiowas, Comanches, and Arapahos to sign up as scouts for the "Great Father," offering soldiers' pay, horses, guns, and blankets—and white officers who would "tell them what we want them to do." In spite of its arrogance, Hancock's speech had a conciliatory tone. His expedition was grinding down to a public failure, but he still believed there were good Indians and bad Indians, and that it was worth the trouble to distinguish between the two.

Kicking Bird then said: "I know you [General Hancock] are a big chief.[1] I heard sometime ago that you were coming, and am glad to see you, and glad you have taken us by the hand. Our great chief, Te-Haw-Son, is dead. He was a great chief for the whites and Indians. Whatever Te-Haw-Son said, they kept in their hearts. Whatever Te-Haw-Son told them in council they remembered, and they would go the road he told them; that is, to be friendly to the whites. Te-Haw-Son always advised the nation to take the white man by the hand, and clear above the elbow. Kicking Bird advises the same. We live south of the river. Kiowas, Comanches, Arapahoes, and Apaches—we all in our hearts want peace with the whites. This country south of the Arkansas is our country. We want peace in it, and not war. We have seen you [General Hancock], and our hearts are glad. We will report the talk you have had with us to all of the nations, so they will know what you have said. When there is no war south of the Arkansas, our women and children can sleep without fear of being molested, and our men can hunt buffalo there without fear of enemies. My heart is big and glad that you have told us that you will not make war on Indians whose consciences are good. We have often wished for the Sioux and Northern Cheyennes not to come down here. They steal our horses when they come here and we do not want them to come. I have heard that our goods are coming early this spring. When they arrive, that will be the time to pick out young men for guides and scouts.

After I get back to my people, I will tell the words you have said to our chiefs, and when it has been told our young men, they will report what they will do. You can see for yourself that we are peaceably encamped on the other side of the river, and no matter what kind of storm comes [alluding to the recent great snow storm], we have stayed to talk with you. Whatever you have to tell, we will listen to, and we know that it is the truth. Now and then, we have robes to trade for sugar and coffee for our women and children. On the prairie, we eat buffalo meat. We are camped close by here."

Hancock responded by saying he wanted an answer about the scouts as soon as possible, to which Kicking Bird replied that he could not give an answer until he talked with the other Kiowa chiefs. Hancock then urged the Kiowas to keep away from Black Kettle's band of Cheyennes, who had separated from the other Cheyennes and gone south. His final advice to Kicking Bird was that his people should settle in their own country and, like the eastern tribes, begin to raise corn and animals.

Kicking Bird could not predict what the young men would do. He, like the Cheyenne chief Black Kettle, was one of the elders who believed their tribes could only survive if they were at peace with the white man. But they could not control their young warriors who would raid settlements for plunder and excitement.

Five days later, on the 28th, at another council, Little Raven, head chief of the Arapahoes, spoke as follows: "We had heard of the Sioux above here, about their going away and leaving their lodge, but for all that, we have come in as fast as our horses could carry us.[2] This route and the Smoky Hill route are free. We don't stop the roads. We love the whites. We made peace with the commissioners from Washington at the mouth of the Little Arkansas, and that peace we have kept for two years.[3] We have a great many brothers and friends in the southern country, and we have sent runners to tell them to listen to what you [General Hancock] have to say. The Sioux in the north do not listen to me, nor the Arapahoes who have lived in the north for years. They do not belong to the nation; they are the same as the Sioux. The commissioners at Washington look to me as the head chief of the Arapahoes. I have told all the Indians of all the nations the same as I tell you, and you sent for me to come and see you, and I came as fast as I could. My heart is glad to see you. We wish you to inform your soldiers on the roads, that we are not with the Sioux and the Cheyennes. We will report what you say to us to all the nations. Whatever you have to say, let it be in plain language so that we can understand it. We do not belong north at all with the Sioux or any other tribe; we belong south. Until the Sioux and Cheyennes go north of the North Platte, we will remain south of the Arkansas. It is a good thing for the soldiers to camp along the different streams, for we can then come in and trade with them. We don't want to stop the railroads at all. Our hearts are glad when we come here with our wives and children and meet all you chiefs with friendship. What you say we will listen to, and when our people come in for their treaty goods we will have a good chance to report to them what you have told us. It is likely that you have heard of Arapahoes committing depredations; that is false. Other Indians have done so, and have laid it to the Arapahoes. All the other villages of our people, save mine, are a great ways off, and that is the reason we came in first. They will all be in. Their lodges are further off south. The Arapahoes, Comanches, Kiowas, Apaches, and Osages are almost all camped at Salt Plains. We hope that you will give provisions to take home with us. We hope that when you go to Washington you will report that Little Raven has a good heart for the whites. The Great Spirit listens and knows that this is true. I am getting old. These young men are my children. I am working hard, myself, for peace. We are glad to meet all of your chiefs, and glad to take you by the hands. We want to know if you have heard of forty animals being taken by us from the whites up the road. Three Cheyennes and three Arapahoes took them. The Arapahoes got twenty-five head and the Cheyennes the remainder."

General Hancock's reply to the Arapahos is consistent in tone and content with his address to the Kiowa chiefs. He describes briefly his troubles with the Sioux and Cheyennes on the Smoky Hill, the burning of the village on the Pawnee

Fork, and his intention to catch and punish individual Indians who murder and rob white men. He invites Arapahos to sign up as scouts for the army and warns them not to molest the roads and railroads, saying that if they do, the "Great Father" will take away the entire country and leave no Indians in it. Clearly, Hancock's declarations were offensive to Isaac Coates. Some parts of the speech were certainly intended to impress and intimidate the Indians as Isaac says, but other parts carry more conciliatory messages. Hancock says twice that he does not want to bring his troops so close to the Indian villages that he would scare off the women and children, a remarkable statement for the general to make only two weeks after he had disregarded the advice of Colonel Wynkoop and camped near the village on the Pawnee Fork. He repeats what he said to the Sioux and Cheyenne chiefs, that he did not come to make war but to find out "who wished for war and who desired peace. If any tribes wish for war, we will fight them. If they wish for peace, we will treat them as friends. Your Great Father at Washington and all his soldiers are friends of the Indian as well as of the white man, but the Indians must not murder and commit other depredations; and they must give up those of their tribe for trial who commit such depredations hereafter."[4]

Later in the year, Hancock was replaced, and the Indians would hear few expressions of friendship from the fire-breathing Sheridan. By December of 1868, Sheridan was writing to Sherman that he planned to hang his hostages, Kiowa chiefs Lone Wolf and Satanta, at sunrise "to the nearest tree" if the Kiowas did not come in immediately and submit to "severe" punishment. Sheridan said that he had made "no pretence to be friendly disposed" and that everything he had asked was in the form of a demand because they were "a few thieving, treacherous chiefs of predatory bands of savages backed up and encouraged by unprincipled and designing Indian agents."

General Hancock replied in a long speech, now with friendly sentiments, now with declarations intended to impress on the Indians an exalted idea of our military strength, and thereby, to intimidate them. He was replied to by Little Raven, but I will go on now to give the finest specimen of Indian "talk" which happened during the expedition. It was at a

council held at Fort Larned, Kansas, May 1st, 1867, between General
Hancock and Satanta, chief of the Kiowas.[5] Satanta said:

"I look upon you and General Smith as my fathers. I want friends, and
I say by the sun and the earth I live on, I want to talk straight and tell the
truth. All the other tribes are my brothers, and I want friends, and am
doing all I can for peace. If I die first, it is all right. All of the Indians south
of here are my friends. When I first started out as a warrior, I was a boy;
now I am a man, and all men are my friends. I want the Great Father at
Washington and all his soldiers and troops to hold on. I don't want the
prairies and country to be bloody; but just hold on for a while. I don't want
war at all; I want peace. As for the Kiowas talking war, I don't know anything about it; nor do I know anything about the Comanches, Cheyennes
and Sioux talking about war. The Cheyennes, Kiowas and Comanches are
poor. They are all of the same color. They are all red men. This country
here is old, and it all belongs to them. But you are cutting off the timber,
and now the country is of no account at all. I don't mean anything bad by
what I say. I have nothing bad hidden in my breast at all. Everything is all
right there. I have heard that there are many troops coming out in this
country to whip the Cheyennes, and that is the reason we were afraid and
went away. The Cheyennes, Arapahoes and Kiowas heard that there were
troops coming out in this country, so also the Comanches and Apaches,
but did not know whether they were coming for peace or war. They were
on the lookout and listening and hearing from down out of the ground all
the time. They were afraid to come in. I don't think the Cheyennes
wanted to fight, but I understand that you burned their village. I don't
think that is good at all. To you, General, and to all these officers sitting
around here, I say that I know that whatever I tell you will be sent to
Washington, and I don't want anything else but the truth told. Other
chiefs of the Kiowas, who rank below me have come in to look for rations
and to look about, and their remarks are reported to Washington, but I
don't think their hearts are good. [That is that some other chiefs come in
and talk simply to get something to eat.]

"Lone Wolf, Stumbling Bear, —— Wolf, and Kicking Bird all come in with that object and their speeches amount to nothing. The Cheyennes, the Arapahoes, the Comanches, Kiowas, Apaches, and some of the Sioux all sent to see me, for they know me to be the best man, and sent information that they wanted peace. They do not work underhanded at all, but declare plainly that they want peace. I hope that you two Generals [Hancock and Smith] and all these officers around here will help the Cheyennes and not destroy them, but let them live. All of the Indians south of this desire the same, and when they talk that way to me, I give them praise for it. Whatever I hear in this council and whatever you tell me, I will repeat when I reach my villages; and there are some Cheyennes over there whom I will tell, and will induce them to preserve peace; but if they will not listen to me, all of my men and myself will have nothing more to do with them. I want peace and will try to make them keep peaceful. The Kiowas braves have grown up from childhood, obtaining their medicine from the earth. Many have grown old, and continue growing old, and dying from time to time, but there are some remaining yet. I do not want war at all but want to make friends, and am doing the best I can for that purpose.

"There are four different bands of Comanches camped at different points in the south, along on the streams, and there are five different bands of Kiowas—those of Lone Wolf, Heap of Bears, Timber Mountain, and Stumbling Bear and they profess to be chiefs, although they have but two or three lodges each. They are waiting, however, to hear what they can learn before taking the war path. The Kiowas do not say anything, and whatever the white man says is all right for them. The Kiowas and the white men are in council today, but I hope no mistake will be made about what the Indians say here, and that nothing will be added to it, because I know everything is sent right to Washington."

GENERAL HANCOCK: "There are two or three interpreters here to witness and prevent mistakes in the translation, so that all will be properly written down."

SATANTA: "About 2 o'clock, I want to start back to Fort Dodge and I want
   you to give me a letter."

GENERAL HANCOCK: "As soon as I can copy it, I will give you the written proceedings of this council, but cannot say that I can give it to you
   as soon as that."

SATANTA: "I simply want a letter when I go into camp, so that I can show
   it."

GENERAL HANCOCK: "I will give you a copy of the proceedings to take
   with you, so that you may show it to any man who may be able to read
   it to you."

Satanta continued: "As for the wagon road, I have no objection to it,
but I don't want any railroad here, but upon the Smoky Hill route, a railroad can run there and it is all right. On the Arkansas and all those northern streams, there is no timber, it has all been cut off; but nevertheless if
anybody knows of anything bad being done [by the Indians], I do not like
it. There are no longer any buffalo around here nor anything we can kill to
live on; but I am striving for peace now, and don't want anything con-
strued to be bad from what I say, because I am simply speaking the plain
truth. The Kiowas are poor. Other tribes are very foolish. They make war
and are unfortunate, and then call upon the Kiowas to aid them, and I
don't know what to think about it. I want peace and all of these officers
around this country know it; I have talked with them until now I am tired.
I came down here and brought my women with me, but came for peace.
If any white men steal our stock, I will report it openly. I continue to come
often and am not tired. Now I am doing the best I can, and the white man
is looking for me. If there were no troops in this country, and the citizens
only lived around here, that would be better, but there are so many troops
coming in here that I fear they will do something bad to me. When Satank shot the sentinel here at the post some two or three years since, there
was then war and that was bad; I came near losing my life then. The
Kiowas have thrown him [Satank] away. If the Indians up north wish to
act foolishly, that is not any of my business, and is no reason why we

should do so down here. If the Indians further south see the white man coming, they will not come upon the war path nor fight. They will not do so if they want to fight, but will call a council and talk as they do here now. Today it is good, and tonight it is good; and when the grass comes [for their ponies], it will be good; and this road which runs up to the west is good also. Everything is all right now. If you keep the horses herded around here, close to the fort, they will never be good. Let them run away off on the prairies. There is no danger; let them get grass, and they will get fat. But do not let the children and boys run away off on the hills now. That is not good; I don't do it, nor do the Cheyennes. I think that is a very good idea. You [Hancock] are a very big chief; but when I am away over to the Kiowas, then I am a big chief myself. Whenever a trader comes to my camp, I treat him well, and do not do anything out of the way to him. All the traders are laughing and shaking hands with me. Whenever the Indians get a little liquor, they get drunk, and fight sometimes and sometimes they whip me, but when they get sober, they are all right, and I don't think anything about it. All the white men around here can look at me and hear what I say; I am doing all I can to keep my men down and doing the best I can to have peace. Down at the mouth of the Little Arkansas, where a treaty was made, Colonel Leavenworth was present.[6] I was the first man that came in here to make peace with Colonel Leavenworth, and I did it by my word. Little Mountain, the former chief of the tribe, is now dead. He did all he could to make peace and kept talking and talking, but the white man kept doing something bad to him, and he was in so much misery that he died. The white man and Indians kept fighting each other backward and forward, and I came in and made peace myself. Little Mountain did not give me my commission, I won it myself. These here braves [pointing to some Indians around him] are chiefs also, and are not afraid of soldiers, and the sight of them does not frighten them at all. This prairie is large and good and so are the heavens above, and I do not want them stained by the blood of war. I don't want you to trouble yourself, and have fear about bringing out too many trains in this country, for I don't want to see any wagons broken or destroyed by war. Now I want to find

out what is the reason Colonel Leavenworth did not give me some annuity goods. I have never talked bad, and I don't want to talk bad, but want
to find out the reason why I did not get my annuity goods. Here are Lone
Bear, Heap of Bears, Stumbling Bear, and Little Heart, and others, six
chiefs with very small bands, and they all received their annuity goods,
while those of my tribe are as plenty as the grass, and I came in for my
goods and did not see them. You can look upon us all, and see if any of us
have those goods; all we have, we have bought and paid for. We are all
poor men, and I think others have got all the goods, but let them keep
them. I want peace, and I don't want to make war on account of our
goods. I expect to trade for what I get, and not get anything by making
speeches. My heart is very strong. We can make robes and trade them.
That is what we have to live upon. I have no mules, horses nor robes to
give Colonel Leavenworth for my goods. I am a poor man, but I am not
going to get angry and talk about it."

*Here, Satanta insinuates to Hancock that Leavenworth might be profiting per-
sonally from the delivery of government treaty goods.*

"I simply want to tell this to these officers present. Such articles of
clothing as the white man may throw away, we will pick up and brush off
and use, and make out the best we can; and if you throw away any provisions, we will clean and use them also, and thus we do the best we can. I
see a great many officers around here with fine clothing, but I do not
come to beg. I admire fine clothes, although I never did beg for anything
of that sort; I have no hat and am going without one, the same as all the
other Kiowas. Colonel Bent used to come over often to my tent, and the
Kiowas went there to him very often, and were glad and shook hands with
him, and Mr. Curtis went there, and he was treated the same way. All
were treated the same, but I am not poor enough to die yet. I think my
women can make enough to live upon, and can make something yet.
When Colonel Bent was our agent and brought our goods out to us, he
brought them out and kept them in a train, and when he arrived, he un-

loaded all our goods to us, and that was the way to do it. But now there is a different way of doing things. At my camp, I waited and sent for the agent, and did not see him, but other chiefs mounted their horses and went there and claimed to be principal men.

"I heard that the railroad was to come up through this country, and my men and other tribes objected to it, but I advised them to keep silent. I thought that by the railroad being built up through here, we would get our goods sure, but they do not come. I would like to get some agent who is a good and responsible man, one that would give us all our annuities; I do not want an agent that will steal half our goods and hide them, but an agent who will get all my goods and bring them out here and give them to me. I am not talking anything badly or angrily, but simply the truth. I don't think the great men at Washington know anything about this, but I am now telling you officers to find it out. Now I am done and whatever you [General Hancock] have to say to me, I will listen to, and those who are with me will listen, so that when we return to camp, we can tell all the others the same as you tell us."

Colonel Leavenworth made an explanation in regard to Satanta's criticisms of him; stating that the goods were withheld because Satanta had not come up to certain stipulations. General Hancock made a very long speech, closing with an explanation that when the wood was gone the Indian, like the white man, could use coal, which was as good if not better. And the speech of Satanta made such a favorable impression on the General that he gave the Indian orator one of his coats, with the full insignia of major general on it, together with a plumed military hat, and yellow sash.

One has to wonder how much of what Satanta said about picking up and dusting off used clothing was a genuine appeal and how much was melodrama calculated to produce whatever windfall might turn up. (Coming from one of the most resolute and audacious warrior chiefs on the southern plains, the bit about not having any hat sounds particularly disingenuous.) And the windfall did arrive, in the form of the major general's uniform, complete with plumed hat and silk sash.

It was reported of Satanta that, on the first of June following, while donned in this major general's uniform, he ran off all the stock at Fort Dodge. But I never heard the report confirmed, and the soldiers and plainsmen are such abominable falsifiers, when speaking of the Indians, that it is difficult to believe anything they say. So I give Satanta the benefit of the doubt.

Isaac Coates was so impressed by Satanta's eloquence that he underestimated his creativity. Davis says that after Satanta stampeded the stock at Fort Dodge, he not only raised his plumed hat to the garrison of the fort but shook his major general's coattails as he rode away. In an earlier escapade several years before, Satanta is reported to have shot a guard at Fort Larned, chased off the fort's horses, and then a few days later sent the post commander a message complaining of the poor quality of the horses.

I have purposely devoted considerable space to Indian oratory, for the reason that it is the scarcest of all kinds of literature, and therefore curious and interesting. In a few years, the savage red men will have passed away, and while we yet may, we should diligently gather everything of interest relating to them. All Indian oratory is remarkable for its simplicity and brevity of expression; and, very frequently, as in the case of Satanta's, for elevated and dignified sentiment as well as for the sublime and pathetic.

If, from the brain of an untutored savage, such intellectual scintillations radiate, what irradiation might we not justly anticipate from it after subjection to civilization, culture and refinements. Indian philology hereafter (when these people shall have passed away) will form an interesting chapter in the history of language; and may give the ethnologist a key to unlock the mystic past and determine the link these people hold in the chain of nations.

NINE

Waiting at Fort Hays

GENERAL HANCOCK left Larned on the 2nd of May and reached Fort Hays on the afternoon of the 3rd. He found General Custer patiently waiting supplies of subsistence stores and forage. The horses were suffering for want of hay and corn. Scurvy had made its appearance among the men. The Indians that were to have been scared into the submissiveness of setter dogs, were away off on the wide prairies, laughing at our crippled condition; and as completely out of our reach and harm's way, as the eagle that builds his nest among the beetling cliffs of the Rocky Mountains.

General Hancock started for the east, and civilization, again on the 5th, taking with him Battery B, 4th U.S. Artillery. I never was a Major General Commanding; but I think I can imagine the feelings of supreme disgust, chagrin and mortification that the failure of this expedition had entailed upon General Hancock. The expedition as it started out exhibited a good deal of the "pride, pomp and circumstance of glorious war." It had been heralded, from the New York dailies to every village weekly, throughout the land. It was to intimidate the Indians into promise of good behavior, and to warn them against scaring our officers at the various military posts on the Plains by their jocular bravado of future hostilities—our officers were not to be frightened!—and in case of war the red savages were to be cut down like grass before the mower's scythe. Thus the papers pictured it. And Theodore R. Davis, one of Harper's most accomplished artists, was along to illustrate the history of the expedition with all the skill of his facile and dexterous pencil.

General Hancock's expedition on the Plains was to end forever all our Indian troubles. In his own words: "It was to show the Indians that we are able to chastise any tribes who may molest people travelling across the Plains"; but it turned out we were not able to do anything of the kind. The General's intention was to use the force of argument rather than the argument of force. Like Hamlet to his mother the General was going to "speak daggers to the Indians but use none."

But then the Indians did not understand this—for which piece of ignorance or stupidity they were manifestly culpable, being savages—and then the General's personification of "grim-visaged war" contrasted strangely with his declarations of peace. In their eyes, the General's coming, like the ghost of Hamlet's father, was "in such a questionable shape" that they were (inspired by the instinct of self-preservation) inclined to ask with Hamlet:

"Be thou a spirit of Hell, or goblin damned, Bring with thee airs from Heaven or blasts from Hell: Be thy intentions wicked or charitable?"

But finding they would be left to "burst in ignorance," they acted Falstaff's chief military maxim, that "discretion is the better part of valor." And when the cage (the Indian village) was examined, lo! the bird was flown.

The command had been in the field six weeks, was already crippled and disabled, and had accomplished no more than that King of France who "marched up the hill, and then marched down again." Nor was General Hancock to blame though the New York dailies and village weeklies all over the land, howled and bellowed with disappointed rage over the failure of the expedition. The General had been sent out to do what could not be done; to deal with savage men as though they were civilized. To march an army—in their eyes a very porcupine of Mars—into their very midst, when they were pregnant with a thousand fears and alarms, from the remembrance of recent past treacheries and massacres, suffered at the hands of the whites.

The only criticism that can be justly made against the General is that he did not exercise that good common sense and military discretion in this expedition, which characterized him during the Rebellion, and which will always give him a distinguished place among great men of America, while history of that war continues to be read.

Before leaving for Fort Leavenworth, General Hancock "very affably favoured" Stanley with his views of the expedition. Stanley then summarized his own impressions: "Congress voted $150,000 to pay the expenses of this short campaign. The troops have marched over 450 miles. The guilty tribes—viz., the Sioux and Cheyennes—have been separated from their ancient allies, the Kiowas, Arapahoes, and Comanches. One hundred thousand dollars' worth of property has been burnt, and the guilty tribes have been despoiled of everything save their horses, squaws, and papooses. The wigwam poles lately burned cannot be replaced without going to the mountains, which will involve them in war with their hated enemies, the Utes. The Santa Fe and Smoky Hill routes will in future be better guarded. Kansas is now free from all hostile Indians, and is open to the emigrant. Briefly, that is all the expedition has accomplished. Of one thing we are certain, Major General Hancock obeyed his orders to the very letter."[1]

The failure of the quartermaster's department to have hay and forage (grain) waiting at Fort Hays for General Custer's horses was a serious blow to the expedition. General Hancock described it in official correspondence as "a matter of supreme regret, and a great injury to the public service." Custer thought his position was "not only embarassing but mortifying" because he was unable to continue his pursuit of the Indians. The grass was not yet up, and the Indian ponies were the weakest they would be until the next winter. Custer might have been able to catch them in camp on the Solomon Fork and finish the job, but he was stuck at Fort Hays. Hancock was frustrated in his goal of showing force to the Kiowas and Comanches because he could not move his cavalry south of the Arkansas until he had adequate forage for his own worn-out horses. It was bad enough that impassable roads and high water had prevented delivery of the necessary supplies, but what was unforgivable to Hancock and Custer was the apparent dereliction of Captain Bradley, the expedition's quartermaster, in not advising Hancock of the problem. If Hancock had known in advance that the forage had not reached Fort Hays, he would have sent Custer to another fort.

May was a bad time for the Seventh Cavalry. Hanging around Fort Hays gave the men plenty of time to think about how bored they were and how terrible the food was. Desertions, always high in the Seventh Cavalry, reached fifty a month, and the deserters usually got away with their horses, arms, and other equipment. Custer said that in one year, one regiment lost more than half of its effective force to desertion. Davis attributed the persistent desertions to the then-common practice of enlisting in the army under an assumed name for a free trip to see the country and leaving when something better came along, like working in the mines or cutting railroad ties for the Union Pacific Railroad. Custer blamed much of the problem on the food, citing instances when the men were served bread that had been baked in 1861. But Custer himself caused some of the dissatisfaction in the ranks. Robert Utley writes that frustration and longing for his wife brought out "the petulant boy" in Custer. Captain Barnitz, a former wartime comrade and admirer of Custer, said that he had become "the most complete example of a petty tyrant" that he had seen.[2] Isaac Coates, always loyal to his friend the general, does not mention troubles in morale, saying only that "scurvy prevailed to a frightful extent." When the antiscorbutics did not come, the men organized buffalo hunts to obtain fresh meat, which Isaac thought "a good substitute for vegetables." The men really needed vegetables and fruit, even wild green plants, and it is doubtful that buffalo meat had any effect at all as an antiscorbutic, but fresh meat must have been a welcome addition to the menu.

When Custer arrived at Fort Hays, only one or two days' supplies of hay and forage were available for his exhausted horses. Isaac Coates thought that the animals were "fairly broken down" from hard, long days and nights on the march and would need several weeks of rest. Stanley wrote on May 9 that the horses were "in a very poor condition from lack of forage" and were dying at the rate of four or five a day. On May 1, however, Hancock had written Sherman from near Fort Larned that, despite reports to the contrary, the expedition's animals were not suffering and had plenty of grain, but very little hay. He also said that he "presumed" that Custer was already out operating against the Cheyennes and Sioux. Much to Hancock's irritation, however, the Seventh Cavalry was not out chastising Indians but, instead, at Fort Hays, resting the horses, hunting buffalo, running footraces, battling scurvy, and losing men daily by desertion.

Moreover, General Custer, although renowned for his impetuosity, showed no signs of stirring from Fort Hays and would not for another month, when he judged the spring grass to be ready for his horses. Isaac Coates helped Custer while away the time by lending him books, including volumes of poetry and Origin of the Stars.

On May 7, Captain Mitchell, Hancock's adjutant, wrote from Fort Harker to General Smith, saying that forty-five thousand rations of subsistence were at Fort Harker bound for Fort Hays, and a supply of forage would leave for Fort Hays on May 8. "In view of these facts, the major general commanding wishes you to make an expedition at the earliest possible day, with the cavalry at Fort Hays, or with that portion of it which may be in condition to move, against all Sioux and Cheyenne Indians who may be found between the Arkansas and Platte Rivers." According to Davis, Custer did make one brief foray into the field sometime before May 31, an unsuccessful overnight search for Indians he had been told were near Lookout Station, but nothing came of it, and he does not even mention the incident in My Life on the Plains. *Another factor that may have increased Custer's reluctance to leave until the grass was up and all the men and horses were ready was Libbie's arrival at Fort Hays on May 17.*

While the cavalry was engaged in protracted preparations at Fort Hays, Indians were attacking ranches and stage stations along the Platte and harassing and killing working parties of the Union Pacific Railroad. Telegrams reporting raids and murders, and asking for more troops, passed back and forth between generals Hancock and Sherman, and Brevet Major General C. C. Augur, commander of the Department of the Platte; from General Grenville Dodge of the Union Pacific Railroad; and from representatives of Wells, Fargo & Co. The call was for more cavalry as quickly as possible. The American Express Company gave instructions to its employees to shoot any Indian who came "within shooting distance."

In the East, the administration was under intense political pressure to do something to restore confidence in the military and gain control of what was obviously a full-blown Indian war on the plains. Custer's leisurely preparations for a spring campaign were embarassing enough, but, even worse, the New York dailies and village weeklies were still, as Isaac put it, howling and bellowing about "Hancock's War." In an effort to repair the damage, Grant sent Hancock a bundle of fifteen letters and reports relating to the expedition, and asked for his comments. On the same day, May 23, Grant also sent Hancock a telegram requesting an immediate explanation of Hancock's burning of the Indian village. Hancock acknowledged receiving the wire but waited until July 31, more than two months after receiving Grant's request, to comment officially on the letters and reports. Both he and Grant knew that whatever Hancock said would become public immediately and would be distributed around the country by the newspapers. Hancock devoted much of his response to refuting statements made in Wynkoop's March and April reports to his superiors in the Office of Indian Affairs. Since Wynkoop was writing his official reports on the scene at the time the events were taking place, however, they have the ring of conviction. Some of Hancock's rejoinders, on the other hand, must have raised eyebrows, both because they stretch the limits of logic and sound so defensive. Taken altogther, Hancock's July letter could not have been a great help to Grant.

In September, Wynkoop sent off an impassioned letter to Superintendent of Indian Affairs Thomas Murphy, which was also published in newspapers and periodicals around the country. Wynkoop's courteous, analytical response could have been devastating to the credibility of Hancock's official explanation of his actions, except that Wynkoop, who had a somewhat mixed reputation, was taking on one of the more admired men in the United States.

Every preparation was now being made to patch up the command and get it ready for another campaign. The red savages were to be taught that the military had not only the weapons of Mars but the agility and speed of Mercury. The Europeans had complained that the First Napoleon didn't fight according to the rules—the army was making the same complaint—the Indians were to be compelled to fight by rule, hereafter. The army wasn't going to stand any military nonsense from savages.

General A. J. Smith (commanding the district) remained at Fort Hays to facilitate our departure. We had all our scouts and guides, and the brave couriers who had been sent with dispatches. These last had been chased for miles by Indians, and narrowly escaped with their lives; but finally, almost exhausted from fatigue, reached General Hancock in safety, and returned with him. Everything seemed to conspire to detain us. The spring had been very backward, with cold rains which still continued. The grass was only sprouting, and, for some weeks yet would not suffice for the horses without hay or corn. And then the horses were fairly broken down, and must have several weeks of rest, with plenty of forage and good care, before they would be able for a campaign. And last, the scurvy prevailed to a frightful extent. Throughout the whole command, not more than one man in ten was free from it. The antiscorbutics did not come. There was nothing left to do but get up hunting parties for buffalo, whose meat is a good substitute for vegetables in the scurvy.

About fifteen miles north of us lay the Saline, a beautiful stream—with now and then a brackish taste as it coursed through salty marshes or banks—where the buffalo were already grazing on the new grass. The hunt we had had on the march from the Indian village to the Smoky Hill had given me an appetite for this wild sport, and had fired me with an ambition to become "a mighty hunter." Every novice sportsman is ambitous for success on his first hunt. In a great hunt in the cypress swamps of Louisiana in 1859, while a guest of my friend Dr. William R. Ulrich of that state, I had had the good fortune to kill the first wild deer I ever saw.

In the last hunt, there were but a few buffalo started by accident, and I rather a spectator than hunter, since I was some distance off when the chase commenced, and got in only at the death—seeing but the two buffalo that had already received their fatal wounds. So I was still hopeful of realizing my wishes on my first hunt; and to accomplish as much with the buffalo as I had with the deer. The party was finally made up, composed of Lieutenant Mayland Cook, Major Harrow, myself, and several others. Two four-horse ambulances to bring in the meat accompanied us—following at a short distance. We were on our way before the sun had risen. A buffalo hunt was new to most of us, and it was amusing to the old hunters to hear the novices discussing, with an air of confidence, the havoc they would make on the buffalo, how they would ride up to the first one and put in a fatal shot, and then dash on to another and slay him, and so on, until in their imagination, they had the plains strewn with game. After a ride of ten miles, we made the ascent of a little hill from the summit of which, a mile distant in the valley below, we saw twelve or fifteen buffalo grazing. As generals in consultation before a battle, so we. The plan was agreed upon. It was in accordance with the highest military teaching. The center was to be charged, and immediately after the right and left wings. The ambulances were halted that their white covers might not scare the buffalo. We were all ready; the word was given. The spurs went in deep; and from the jump we went down that hill and across the plain at a frightful pace. In ten minutes—notwithstanding we had been discovered and the game was fleeing—we were in the midst of the buffalo, going pell mell, every man now for his game. My fiery little horse took fright and ran away with me. Everybody was firing in every direction. The bullets were whizzing through the air all about, making horrid music; bringing out every now and then a yell, "Don't shoot this way!" "Lookout! Lookout! Be careful where you are shooting!" But nobody heeded the warnings. A hunter whose blood is boiling with excitement from the chase has annihilated prudence. He has but one idea. He shoots wildly or dashes on furiously, exclaiming: "A buffalo! A buffalo! My kingdom for a buffalo!" My horse was finally reined up after running a mile. Everybody by this time was widely scattered. My horse was wild with fear, and I now realized the necessity of training him for the hunt. I put my carbine in the holster, arranged my spurs, tightened the girth, and dashed away for a couple of buffalo more than a mile off. As I came up near them, my horse reared and jumped and snorted, like a newly lassoed mustang. He was terrified, and dashed away again for several hundred yards. My task was a little like an aquatic sportsman attempting to sail his yacht against the wind. I bouted ship again, and brought my little French Canadian down on the fleeing twain; this time getting a little nearer; then sheering away for a hundred yards; then coming up again, each tack coming nearer to my game, until, after a chase of five miles, I was enabled to get within fifteen or twenty yards. The buffalo were just now beginning the ascent of a long and pretty steep hill. This was decidedly to my advantage. The buffalo are

very heavy in front, and light behind, making their ascent of a hill difficult
and slow; giving the horse here great advantage, who climbs a hill rapidly.
There was not a living thing in sight but the buffalo. The Indians might
be just over the hill, or in some deep ravines lying across our path, and
then—a very common thing, indeed—I might get lost.

I was fairly inebriated with the sport, and as wildly, as insanely anxious
as a gambler who has staked his last dollar. I drew the carbine very carefully—I had five minutes yet; for, the summit gained, the buffalo would
go down the hill as fast as I—as I cocked the gun, I put a spur on the
right, got fairly abreast and within fifteen yards, dropped the reins on the
horse's neck, took aim with both hands, and pulled the trigger. My horse
leaped into the air, stumbled, plunged and dashed ahead of the buffalo
who did not change his course. I saw the blood streaming from his mouth
as I looked backward over my left shoulder. The shot had been fatal, the
ball passing through the right lung into the region of the heart and cutting
off some of the large blood vessels centering there. Exhausted from weakness, the buffalo paused a moment, of which I took advantage, dismounted and put another ball just behind the foreshoulder. The poor
brute staggered on for a few paces with a crimson stream pouring from
his protruding tongue and issuing from his expanded nostrils, then fell
with a headlong plunge, to the ground and expired in a moment. My ambition—through this cruel piece of work—was satisfied, and with a satis-
faction which might better become a savage Indian, bellowed out with
Caesar, VENI, VIDI, VICI!

The Rest of the Story

TEN

Hard Fights and
Long Marches

ALTHOUGH ISAAC COATES ended his journal abruptly with his slaying of the buffalo, the expedition went on—and the repercussions from it lasted longer still.

On June 1, 1867, six companies of the Seventh Cavalry, under the temporary command of Major Wickliffe Cooper, left camp near Fort Hays and marched up the valley of Big Creek. The two remaining companies were left at Fort Hays with General Smith. One of them, Troop G, was under the command of Captain Barnitz, whose wife, Jennie, had arrived in camp late in May. General Smith's plan was for the regiment to travel north to Fort McPherson on the Platte River, then west along the Platte and south to the headwaters of the Republican, then north again to Fort Sedgwick, where the command would pick up supplies, then south to Fort Wallace, and, finally, back to Fort Hays, a total distance of about one thousand miles. Isaac Coates was the expedition medical officer as far as Fort Wallace, where he remained with elements of the command ordered to garrison the post. General Custer stayed on at Fort Hays for the rest of June to arrange for the comfort of Libbie and her young lady friend and to "superintend the locating of their tents." Then, after midnight, Custer and his party of two soldiers, one scout, and four Delaware guides set out on a "moonlight gallop" to catch up with his command, which they did just as reveille was sounding the next morning.[1]

Davis, who accompanied the expedition for the entire trip, thought the country between Fort Hays and Fort McPherson "one of the most interesting portions of the Plains," filled with bluffs and canyons, and traversed by small streams, with banks "fringed with trees of all descriptions, ash and walnut being as plentiful as the cotton-wood." Many of these groves were sacred Indian burial places, but they were also convenient sources of firewood for army wood contractors, who proceeded to cut down the trees. Understandably, this destruction infuriated the Indians.

The column worked its way north, camping each night on one of the many streams that cross the prairies between the Smoky Hill and the Platte. They reached the Republican River on June 6 after an uneventful march—except for the night they had camped in a rattlesnake den. Apparently no one was hurt, and the many rattlesnakes that objected to the intrusion were fried or broiled for breakfast. No Indians were seen on the way. On June 7, however, thirty or forty warriors appeared on a hill a few miles away from the column. Two companies of cavalry started in pursuit but gave up when they found that the war party was mounted on excellent horses, recently stolen from the stage company.

On June 8, an event occurred that shocked the officers and, years later, was to cause Isaac Coates serious trouble. Major Wickliffe Cooper, an alcoholic, shot himself in the head, perhaps in a drunken stupor or because he had run out of liquor. He was found in his tent, covered with blood and with his revolver at his side. Isaac Coates made an official examination of the body, and certified that the cause of death was suicide. His subsequent willingness to help Cooper's widow would end his army career.

Ten days and 215 miles after leaving Fort Hays, the expedition reached Fort McPherson. A few days later, the command moved camp to a site about twelve miles from the fort, near Jack Morrow's ranch. Indian attacks on stagecoaches and ranches continued on the overland road. Davis wrote that there were abandoned ranches all along the Platte and many fresh graves. On the thirteenth, General Custer held a council with Sioux chiefs led by the ubiquitous Pawnee Killer, who, after trying unsuccessfully to discover where Custer was going next, blithely assured him that the Sioux desired to live in peace with their white brothers. As they departed, General Custer presented the Sioux with generous gifts of coffee and sugar. Isaac Coates, who undoubtedly witnessed the conference, must have thought about it when he examined the bodies of Lieutenant Kidder and his ten companions, whom Pawnee Killer murdered and mutilated two weeks later. In Custer's words, the command had seen "no real Indian warfare" up to that time, but they were "soon to experience it, attended by all its frightful barbarities."[2] General Sherman arrived at Fort McPherson the day after the council. He told Custer that he did not trust Pawnee Killer, and doubted his comforting assurances.

On June 18, the expedition headed south over rough, broken country, winding its way through deep canyons and high cliffs to the forks of the Republican River, where they went into camp about seventy-five miles southeast of Fort Sedgwick and about the same distance northeast of Fort Wallace. Custer had specific orders from General Sherman to return to Fort Sedgwick for supplies after scouting the Republican River country. When he arrived at the forks of the Republican River, Custer decided that "circumstances seemed to favor a modification of this plan." Instead of taking the entire command back to Fort Sedgwick over terrain "almost impassable for heavily-laden wagons," he would send a detachment to Fort Wallace for supplies. The road to Fort Wallace was "generally level and unbroken."[3] Since he needed Sherman's approval for the change in plans, he sent Major Joel Elliot, with a guide and ten picked men, back to Fort Sedgwick with dispatches. Elliot and his party set out on the night of June 23, moving as fast as possible in the darkness until they were outside the ring of Indians thought to be watching the camp. On the same day, Lieutenant Robbins left camp with sixteen wagons and a strong escort heading south for Fort Wallace, guided by Medicine Bill Comstock.

A cynical view of Custer's decision suggests that he was more concerned about a letter he had written to Libbie from Fort McPherson inviting her to come to Fort Wallace than he was about the cliffs and canyons of the trail back to Fort Sedgwick. The letter had never actually arrived, but Custer did not know this, and thought Libbie might be waiting for him at

Fort Wallace. He therefore sent another letter to Libbie at Fort Wallace under the care of Colonel William Cooke, "an intimate family friend," asking her to come to the camp on the Republican River (the place, incidently, where Custer and Sherman had agreed the Indians were likely to be concentrated). After thinking about it further, Custer realized that the Indians might wait to attack the train until its return trip from Fort Wallace, when the wagons would be loaded with all the goods the Indians wanted most. Libbie would also be on board. Stirred by "a deeper and stronger motive" than the safety of Lieutenant Robbins and his wagon train, Custer sent off Lieutenant Colonel Myers with a squadron of cavalry to support Colonel Robert West and his troops, who were already in the field, to act as additional escort to the wagon train. Libbie was safely back at Fort Riley when all of this was happening, but if she had been at Fort Wallace, she would have had an exciting trip to camp. (She was impressed by the comment of Colonel Cooke, who told her later that he had promised Custer he would shoot her if the Indians attacked.) In Custer's account of these events, there is not the least hint that deploying a major portion of the Seventh Cavalry, around a countryside full of hostile Indians, to arrange a rendezvous with his wife, might be considered a little odd.

At dawn on the twenty-fourth, Indians struck the camp on the Republican and attempted to drive off the horses. One picket was seriously wounded but survived, due, perhaps, to the professional skill of Dr. Coates. The Indians suffered no losses but gained nothing from their efforts except the picket's carbine and ammunition. Custer writes that hundreds of Indians were involved. Grinnell, not an enthusiastic fan of Custer's, claims his account of the engagement is "distorted and exaggerated." The Indians then withdrew to a hill about a mile from camp, where they flashed their signal mirrors, calling in other parties of warriors from all directions. One of the army scouts, named Gay, arranged a conference, a dangerous business for him and the command, since the Indians greatly outnumbered the troopers. "Imagine our surprise" says Custer, that the leader of the Indians turned out to be the "white man's friend," Chief Pawnee Killer, who gave no reason for the attack but assured Custer that "his heart was good." Two other Sioux chiefs present, Thunder-Lightning and The-Man-Who-Walks-Beneath-the-Ground, said that their hearts were good also. During the conversation, the officers noticed that, contrary to agreement, more warriors were casually moving toward Custer's party. At that point, Custer warned Pawnee Killer to stop the advance of his men or the entire command would immediately prepare for an attack. Neither side was able to extract information from the other, and the conference ended with the chiefs rejoining the main body of Indians and the officers returning to camp. Since Sherman had asked Custer earlier to try to visit Pawnee Killer's village, Custer started out immediately to follow the Sioux to their camp, but the Indian ponies were faster than the army horses, and, after several hours, he gave up pursuit. A short time later, a small party of Indians reappeared temptingly near camp. Captain Louis Hamilton set out with his troop to catch them and unconsciously fell into the Indian trap that had worked so well with Captain Fetterman. The Indians slowly withdrew, and the troopers followed. After a while, the Indians divided into two groups, each heading off in a different direction. Captain Hamilton split his troop into two detachments and continued to follow what was now two parties becoming increasingly distant from each other. When the two cavalry units were far enough apart that they would not be able to help each other, several hundred Indians suddenly jumped out of a ravine and attacked both detachments simultaneously.

Isaac Coates had been riding with Hamilton but joined the other unit, under the command of Brevet Lieutenant Colonel Tom Custer, when the command was divided. For some reason, he subsequently became separated from both parties and found himself alone just at the time when Captain Hamilton came under attack. General Custer says that Coates first started toward the troopers and encircling Indians, "casting his lot with his struggling comrades," but half a dozen warriors left the battle and galloped toward him. Isaac Coates turned his horse and headed for camp as fast as his horse could carry him.

Camp and safety were four miles of rough and broken country away, and the Indians were better mounted. When Isaac came within sight of camp, the Indians were almost within arrow range and gaining on him, but they broke off the chase with a parting volley of bullets, knowing that the troopers in camp would have fresh horses and could probably catch them instead. Isaac Coates rode into camp, threw himself on the ground, and, as soon as he could speak, gave the alarm that Captain Hamilton's troopers were surrounded and in great peril. The command immediately saddled up and started to the rescue. Custer reported two warriors killed, several wounded, and no losses in his command.[4]

General Hancock reported to General Sherman on June 16 that the Indians had moved from the Platte to the Smoky Hill road. Fort Wallace had been attacked, and every station garrisoned by troopers, for ninety-five miles east and seventy-five miles west, had been raided an average of four times each. The stage had been attacked five times. By the third week of June, Fort Wallace had become the center of fierce fighting that would continue all summer. On June 21, Indians killed four soldiers in an attempt to run off the fort's horses.

Several days later, Lieutenant Robbins, who had made the trip from camp on the Republican River to Fort Wallace without difficulty, loaded up his wagons and set out on the return trip. On June 26, Indians appeared outside the fort. In an exciting, tautly written account, Captain Barnitz describes the charge of his troop against the Indians and the wild fight that followed, in which his men engaged the enemy "at close quarters, with carbine and sabre." The Indians also charged in a line, like cavalry, instead of circling as they usually did. Barnitz's losses were six killed and six wounded, one mortally. As they always did, the Indians instantly carried off their wounded, which made it impossible for Barnitz to estimate their casualties, but he thought they were at least equal to his own.[5]

On the same day, a force of seven to eight hundred Cheyennes and Sioux attacked the wagon train escorted by Lieutenant Robbins on its way back to the camp on the Republican River. Robbins placed the wagons in two parallel columns, dismounted his men, and put the horses, led by every fourth man, between the columns. The cavalrymen fought on foot in a protective circle around the train and horses. Although greatly outnumbered, the troopers were able to keep moving in a solid, strictly maintained formation, holding their fire until their targets were close and thus conserving their diminishing supply of ammunition for what promised to be a long fight. The battle continued for several hours, the Indians repeatedly charging the column and being met by controlled volleys from the troopers' carbines. The Indians finally withdrew when two companies of cavalry, under the commands of West and Myers, were seen in the distance coming to relieve the wagon train. Army losses were three killed and two wounded. In this fight and in Captain Barnitz's battle earlier that day, the Indians had fought with unwavering ferocity, charging into the fire of repeating carbines, taking casualties, and returning for more. In every skirmish—with escorted stagecoaches, against army posts, and in fully developed battles like those of June 26, in which fifteen or twenty warriors were killed—the Indians were losing warriors they could not replace, but they continued to attack white men whenever they thought they had even a slight chance of success.

Major Elliott returned safely from Fort Sedgwick on June 27, having made much of the two-hundred-mile trip at night. He carried dispatches from General Sherman ordering General Custer to proceed up the North Republican, then north to the Platte to a point near Riverside Station. Also on the twenty-seventh, General Smith reported to General Hancock that Cheyennes, Arapahos, and Kiowas were "out in full force." On the previous day, General Hancock had telegraphed General Sherman, saying that his mounted force was not adequate to clear the Indians out of the area between the Platte and the Arkansas. He asked that Gatling guns be sent to Custer on the Platte by rail. As soon as Lieutenant Robbins pulled into camp with his wagon loads of supplies, Custer's forces were ready to head for the Platte. They marched up the south bank of the North Republican for fifty or sixty miles and then north to the Platte valley. Isaac Coates reported to Surgeon General Barnes on June 30 that he was on the South Fork of the Republican River.

Working its way north, the expedition marched for six days in the scorching heat of the plains. Custer described the seventh day, July 5, as a "painful journey under a burning July sun of sixty-five miles, without a drop of water for our horses or draft animals. This march was necessarily effected in one day, and produced untold suffering among the poor brutes. Many of the dogs accompanying the command died from thirst and exhaustion."[6] Just why the journey had to be made in that fashion is not clear, nor is it evident why Custer did not mention his own men among the "poor brutes." The command lost thirty-five men, more than 10 percent of its strength, by desertion the next day.

When the sun went down on the evening of the fifth, Custer decided to press ahead to the Platte and find a camping site. The command continued to march along by moonlight, while Custer, Isaac Coates, Lieutenant Moylan, and an orderly rode forward at a brisk rate for the next fifteen miles, reaching the river at about eleven o'clock. They selected a camp site on the river bank, tied their horses to sabres stuck in the ground, covered themselves with their saddle blankets and rubber ponchos, and went to sleep. The next morning, they found that the rest of the expedition had come up during the night and camped along the river.

At Riverside Station, Custer learned, to his dismay, that Lieutenant Lyman Kidder of the Second Cavalry had set out on June 29, carrying orders to Custer from General Sherman. Nothing had been heard of Lieutenant Kidder and his escort of ten men for nearly a week. Custer and the other officers feared the worst.

The Road to Fort Wallace

One day after reaching Riverside Station, the command turned around and started south toward Fort Wallace. Custer, a man of extraordinary physical stamina himself, had driven his troops on a brutal march without any compelling reason for doing so. Morale in the Seventh Cavalry had been terrible. Now it was worse. The thirty-five men who deserted at Riverside Station were part of a continuous stream of men leaving the army, some of them because they never intended to make the army a career, others because conditions had become unbearable. Captain Barnitz, a brave and intelligent career officer, thought that Custer was treating his men with inexcusable cruelty. Sooner or later, the price would be paid. It was, on the march south.

During the journey, Custer learned that a third of the force intended to desert at the first opportunity. At noon on July 7, when the command stopped to rest and graze the horses, the first group of deserters left camp and headed north toward the Platte. Seven of the men were mounted, six were on foot. Custer sent Major Elliott and what men he could collect quickly in pursuit of the deserters, with orders to bring their dead bodies back to camp. The men on horseback were able to escape, but Elliott and his men caught up with the others, shot three, and brought all six back to camp under arrest. Later, one of the wounded men died. When the wagon carrying the wounded men came into camp, Isaac Coates approached it, intending to give them medical attention, but Custer ordered him not to care for them at that time. Later in the day, Isaac Coates was permitted to examine their wounds. Some of the charges brought against Custer in his court-martial involved this episode.

Swinging southeast the next day, the column entered "the prickly pear country," which Davis described with awe as a "most gorgeously-colored tapestry carpet of the most brilliant crimson and yellow." Finally out of "the sharp country" two days later, Davis thought that no man would ever want to return there. The party crossed Chief Creek, one of the head-water streams of the Republican, worked its way east along the North Fork of the Republican, and then cut southeast until striking the trail of Lieutenant Robbins's wagon train to Fort Wallace. There, in the old wagon traces, were the fresher tracks of shod army horses. Now they knew that Lieutenant Kidder had come at least that far, but the question remained what had become of him.

The next day, Bill Comstock and the Delaware guides found the muti-lated bodies of Lieutenant Kidder, his ten men, and their Sioux guide, Red Bead, lying in a tight circle at the bottom of a low basin in the valley of Beaver Creek. A war party of Sioux and Cheyennes led by Pawnee Killer had caught Kidder's command in an indefensible position. Riding

along the high ground and firing down onto the troopers, the Indians easily wiped out Kidder and his men in a few minutes. One or more of the
men had been burned to death after being wounded. Custer's account of
the fight suggests that the men fought off the Indians as they rode toward
Beaver Creek and then put up a desperate fight before being overwhelmed. Davis, who drew some grisly pictures of the scene, said there
were no more than a dozen empty cartridge cases on the ground, and so
concluded the men must have been killed quickly. However, the men had
been armed not only with seven-shot, breechloading Spencer carbines,
but also Colt and Remington cap-and-ball revolvers from the Civil War
that did not use brass cartridges. It is possible that they were able to keep
firing for at least a little while using their revolvers instead of their carbines, in which case there would not have been telltale cartridge cases
lying around as evidence. Lieutenant Kidder was twenty-five years old,
and most of his men were younger. Three of them had come from Ireland
and two from Germany, only to end their short lives in a few brief moments of terror. After Isaac Coates examined the bodies—actually severely mutilated parts of bodies—they were buried in a common grave.[7]

On July 13, Custer's command reached Fort Wallace. Isaac Coates
wrote Surgeon General Barnes that he was on duty at the fort, and that
though some of the men had left Fort Hays with scurvy it had disappeared without the use of antiscorbutics. He also said that the command
had traveled more than seven hundred miles after leaving Fort Hays, a
significant comment because he had otherwise never mentioned conditions in the field in his reports. Isaac knew that the men were exhausted
and that the horses were worn out and needed a long rest.

Isaac Coates remained at Fort Wallace for the next two months. He
must have been busy; not only was the fort an island in a land occupied by
an active and very hostile enemy, but cholera was epidemic, and soldiers
were dying daily. The list of men who succumbed to the disease is melan-
choly evidence of how many soldiers of the Seventh Cavalry had come
across the ocean, from Ireland and Germany especially, only to die a miserable death on the western plains. Perhaps some of them were among the

immigrants whom Isaac had watched with amusement and affection on the train from Philadelphia to Chicago in what seemed a very long time before.

Custer wrote that Fort Wallace was in a state of siege. All travel on the Smoky Hill road had ceased, many of the stage stations were abandoned, the mail had stopped, and the fort was running out of food. By implication, the fort was in desperate straits, and relief was imperative. But Custer only wrote his description of conditions at Fort Wallace, and his justification for his actions of the next several days, after he had been found guilty of abandoning his men to go on a private journey. Only two days after arriving at Fort Wallace, without time to rest after the grueling forced march from the Platte, Custer took seventy-five men and whatever horses could still travel and left at sunset for Fort Harker, either to obtain supplies for the beleaguered Fort Wallace, as he claimed later, or to see Libbie at Fort Riley. The court-martial decided on the latter. Isaac Coates would not see his friend, the general, again until September, when Isaac was a witness for the prosecution at Custer's trial. Isaac reported again to General Barnes on July 31 that he was still on duty at Fort Wallace.

While Isaac Coates was tending cholera victims at Fort Wallace, Custer, Louis Hamilton, and their party were racing for Fort Harker. They reached Fort Hays, a distance of 150 miles, in fifty-five hours, "including all halts," as Custer wrote proudly, leaving broken-down horses along the way. At Fort Hays, Custer commandeered two ambulances and four mules and used them to convey himself as well as three companions, colonels Cooke and Tom Custer, and two enlisted men to Fort Harker "while executing an unauthorized journey on private business," as the court-martial charges put it. Captain Hamilton and the balance of the escort were left at Fort Hays for a brief rest. On the way to Fort Hays, another incident had occurred that would become the substance of an additional court-martial charge. Near Downer's Station a small group of men became separated from the main body of the command and was attacked by Indians. Two men were wounded, one of whom was found later to have died. Custer did not pause to rescue the men or recover their bodies but hurried onward toward Fort Harker, Fort Riley, and Libbie. Custer wrote later that a small party of soldiers had halted some distance behind the column "without authority" and had been attacked by Indians. However, Sergeant James Connelly of the Seventh Cavalry testified under oath at the court-martial that Custer had ordered him to take several men, leave the command, and return along the road to find Custer's missing mare and her handler. If Connelly was telling the truth, Custer had knowingly placed the men in danger and then refused to rescue them.

Reaching Fort Harker after midnight on the morning of July 19, Custer woke up Brevet Major General A. J. Smith, his superior officer, who foggily gave Custer permission to proceed to Fort Riley by rail. Later in the morning, when a more clear-headed Smith had had time to think about the situation, he telegraphed Custer to return at once to Fort Harker. General Hancock immediately gave his support to Smith's action. Custer was then ordered to return to Fort Riley and remain under arrest.

In August, General Hancock was replaced by Major General Philip H. Sheridan. At Fort Wallace, the Seventh Cavalry rested and reorganized, and prepared for further scouting expeditions against the Indians, who, as usual, were hard to find. Captain Barnitz wrote Jennie that he had been out looking for Cheyennes amid fearful heat, with prairie fires everywhere in the distance. Even the Smoky Hill River was dry. Isaac Coates went along on at least one of those expeditions since he made his August 31 report to General Barnes from a camp near the Saline River.

On August 25, General Hancock wired General Sherman that Captain George Armes of the Tenth Cavalry had been attacked on the Republican River by a large force of Indians. Captain Armes's command of one company of regular cavalry and two companies of Kansas volunteers fought the Indians for more than a day until retiring with a loss of three killed and thirty-five wounded. As usual, Indian losses were unknown. Earlier in the month, Cheyennes had piled railroad ties across the Union Pacific tracks near Plum Creek and derailed a handcar. One of the crew was shot and scalped, but survived. Shortly thereafter he returned to his home in England. Encouraged by their success with the handcar, the Indians bent up a rail and derailed a freight train, which they then plundered and burned. The engineer and fireman were killed.

Captain Barnitz wrote Jennie on September 13, describing his delicious dinners and saying that he had a "nice mess" composed of Major Elliott, Dr. Coates, lieutenants Jackson and Brewster, and himself. He had been playing chess with Lieutenant Brewster. In August, according to Robert Utley, Isaac Coates was involved in an argument with Captain Edward Myers, whom Utley says was "a somewhat dull-witted officer" with a bad temper. Dr. Coates had released a sick man from duty, but Myers, calling Coates a "god damn fool" ordered the man back to duty.[8] Isaac enjoyed just two weeks of comparative leisure after the August march through Kansas searching for Indians. On September 14, he received orders to report at once to Fort Leavenworth for the court-martial of General Custer. Isaac would never again ride with his friends of the Seventh Cavalry.

In October, two companies of the Seventh Cavalry and two companies of infantry escorted a seven-man peace commission representing the United States government to a conference with Indian leaders at Medicine Lodge Creek, in southern Kansas. After much discussion, the Treaty of Medicine Lodge Creek was signed by the commissioners and some chiefs, among them Bull Bear, Tall Bull, and White Horse, whom Isaac Coates had met on the North Fork of Pawnee Creek in April. The chiefs who signed the treaty represented only part of the Indian bands directly affected by the agreements, however, and it is questionable that they fully understood what they were signing.

ELEVEN

Custer's Court-martial

CUSTER ENTHUSIASTS blame General Hancock and his proxy, General Smith, for bringing supposedly trumped-up charges against Custer in order to shift the blame of a failed campaign from Hancock to his subordinate. Many of Custer's officers would not agree. Barnitz, for example, an old Civil War comrade of Custer's, had come to despise him. He told Jennie that he was delighted that Custer was in serious trouble. Lawrence Frost quotes a letter in his possession, dated September 7, from Lieutenant Charles Brewster to Custer telling him that he could not "count on" any officers to help him except Lieutenant Wallingford and, perhaps, Hamilton. His list of officers who would not support Custer included Elliott, Myers, Coates, Robbins, Barnitz, Commagere, Hale, Jackson, Levey, and Keogh.

Custer's court-martial convened at Fort Leavenworth on September 15. One day before, Isaac Coates had received instructions to travel immediately from Fort Wallace to Fort Leavenworth and appear as a witness for the prosecution. With General Hancock's concurrence, General Smith had brought two principal charges against Custer. The first was that Custer had left his command without proper authority at a time when the command could expect to be engaged in fighting with hostile Indians. The second charge of conduct prejudicial to "good order and military discipline" included three specifications: first, that Custer had taken three officers, seventy-five men, and horses unfit for service on a rapid march from Fort Wallace to Fort Hays for private business, immediately after the long and exhausting march from the Platte; second, that Custer "while executing an unauthorized journey on private business," procured two ambulances and four mules for his trip from Fort Hays to Fort Harker; and third, that he had made no effort to protect the small, detached party of troopers attacked by Indians near Downer's Station or to recover the bodies of the men killed.

An additional charge of conduct to the prejudice of good order and military discipline, with four specifications, was preferred against Custer by Captain Robert West. These were the charges that brought Isaac Coates to Fort Leavenworth. The specifications (greatly simplified) included allegations that Custer had ordered deserters leaving camp on July 7 to be shot without trial, had refused to allow the acting assistant surgeon to give medical attention to the wounded, and had caused the death of Private Charles Johnson, the trooper who was shot while fleeing and eventually died. Through his counsel, Captain Charles Parsons, Custer pleaded not guilty to all charges and specifications.

When the court-martial convened, the members at first fell to wrangling about who ranked whom and who should vote first. The argument was finally settled by telegrams from the secretary of war through the adjutant general. On September 17, Captain Louis Hamilton testified for the prosecution. The next four days were devoted to procedural matters. On the twenty-second, Lieutenant William Cooke testified for the prosecution. On September 23, Dr. Isaac Coates certified that Brevet Major Asbury was suffering from a bilious attack and could not participate as a member of the court. The proceedings were then put off until the twenty-fourth, when the Court heard the testimony of several officers of the regiment. On September 25, Brevet Major General A. J. Smith took the stand for the prosecution. He was followed by First Lieutenant Tom Custer and, finally, by Lieutenant William Cooke.

At 10:00 A.M. on September 26, Isaac Coates was sworn in as a witness for the prosecution. Dr. Coates testified as follows:[1]

Questions by the Judge Advocate

Q. State your name and position in the army.

A. I. T. Coates, Acting Ass't Surgeon U.S.A.

Q. In what command were you in last July.

A. With the 7th Cav.

Q. Were you with the portion of the 7th Cav. on the march between the Platte River and Ft. Wallace in July last.

A. Yes sir.

Q. Who commanded it.

A. Gen. Custer.

Q. On that march do you know of any deserters from the command.

A. I know there were deserters from the command. I also know of some men who deserted.

Q. Do you know of any action taken or orders given in regard to deserters on that march.

A. I know of no orders given in relation to deserters.

Q. Do you know of any action taken in regard to deserters.

A. Yes sir.

Q. State what action was taken in regard to deserters at any time during that march.

A. As far as my memory serves me, on the 7th of July a number of men deserted while the Regiment had halted and some of those deserters were shot—3 of them to my certain knowledge.

Q. Do you know the names of any men who were shot.

A. Johnson was the last name of one of them. Alburger was the name of another, and the other man's name I don't recollect. I believe they called him Barney, and he was a bugler. I don't recollect his last name, though I recollect the man very well.

Q. On what date did this occur.

A. I think on the 7th of July.

Q. Did you see any of those men deserting or attempting to desert.

A. No sir.

Q. When did you first see them.

A. When they were brought in after they had been shot.

Q. Was the command in camp at the time they were brought in.

A. Yes sir.

Q. In what manner were they brought in.

A. In a wagon.

Q. What kind of a wagon.

A. An ordinary Quarter Master's Wagon—a six mule wagon.

Q. When you first saw them did you give them any medical attendance.

A. No sir.

Q. For what reason did you not.

A. When the wagon first came in, I with a number of others started to it. The men generally, of the command started to the wagon. As I was going to it I believe Gen. Custer said to me not to go near those men at that time. I stopped there, just where I stood, of course. I obeyed his order.

Q. How long were those men in the wagon before you gave them medical attendance.

A. I suppose 2 hours.

Q. What kind of medical attendance did you then give.

A. I administered opiates and made them comfortable, just as I should have done on the field of battle.

Q. Did you do anything else besides give them opiates.

A. No sir: in my judgement there was nothing else required. There was a good deal of clothing in the wagon and I am not sure whether any grain sacks or not, but I used every thing in the wagon to make them a soft place so they should be comfortable.

Q. How badly were those men wounded—give the particulars about each man.

A. Barney Tolliver, the Bugler, was wounded by one shot, the ball entered his right arm and passed immediately through making a flesh wound, and entered the arm again and passed up, making a flesh wound. Alburger had one shot through the shoulder, just above the shoulder

blade, making a flesh wound; and another shot in the side between the
5th and 6th or 6th and 7th ribs, running along the ribs for about 3
inches and then coming out again, making a flesh wound. And he was
also struck on the middle finger of his left hand, making a flesh wound.
He was wounded in 3 places. Johnson was wounded in 2 places. He
also had a shot in the side, I think the left side, making a flesh wound.
He was also wounded in the head, the ball entering in the left temple
and coming out below, under the jaw, and passing down into his lungs,
the same ball entering again at the upper part of the chest.

Q. In your judgement was it the same ball.

A. Yes sir, I am positive of that, the distance from where the ball came out
and where it entered again being very slight and was in a direct line.

Q. Did the appearance of the wound show that the ball entered the left
temple.

A. Yes sir, and came out below; there could be no mistake about that.

Q. In what position should you judge he was when he received the
wound.

A. The shooter must have been some distance above him, I should judge.
The shooter must have been mounted, from the ball having taken that
direction.

Q. Did you judge he was standing up or on the ground.

A. He might have been standing up. From the direction of the ball there
is no reason that he must have been on the ground.

Q. How near should you judge him to have been to the person who fired
the shot.

A. From the power of the ball he must have been within 25 yards at least,
and perhaps much nearer.

Q. Was it a pistol shot or otherwise.

A. It was a pistol shot.

Q. How soon after those men were wounded were their wounds dressed,
if dressed at all.

A. I think it was just 2 days after, as far as I recollect.

Q. During that time did those men follow the column.

A. Yes sir.

Q. In what manner.

A. In the wagon.

Q. In the same wagon.

A. Yes sir.

Q. Were there any ambulances with the column.

A. Yes sir.

Q. How many.

A. Two I think.

Q. Why were not those wounded men put in an ambulance as soon as possible.

A. At the time these accidents occurred to the men the ambulances were not there, but in my judgement the men did better in the wagon going along slow. The ambulances were very poor, the springs were weak and all the men who had ridden in them complained of their being very uncomfortable, and I found them so myself, having to ride in them.

Q. Did you regard the wagon as easier than the ambulance.

A. I did sir.

Q. How many medical officers were there in that command besides yourself.

A. None but myself.

Q. In your opinion would it not have been better to have dressed their wounds than to have delayed it.

A. It was impossible to dress them on account of not having fresh water. We had no water but in the buffalo wallows, and it would have been very hurtful to have dressed the wounds with muddy water. That is the reason I did not dress them. I waited 2 days until we came to a stream of clear water—the first we came to.

Q. Has it not been usual to dress gunshot wounds as soon as possible with whatever kind of water can be obtained.

A. Sometimes gunshot wounds don't need dressing. Sometimes they do better by allowing the blood to congeal on them. That was the case in these cases. The hemorrhage was arrested by the gluing of their clothing to the wounds. And there was no more hemorrhage after the first hour or so. The important thing in gunshot wounds is to arrest the hemorrhage, and that was done in these cases.

Q. How far were the wounded men brought.

A. They were brought to Fort Wallace.

Q. What was the result of the wound received by Johnson.

A. That wound was fatal—it resulted in his death.

Q. Did he die from the effects of the wound received on the 7th of July.

A. Yes sir.

Q. When and where did he die.

A. At Fort Wallace. I am not positive when, but I think it was on the 17th of July. I think it was 4 or 5 days after we arrived at Fort Wallace.

Q. You stated that you administered opiates and made the men as comfortable as possible; how many times did you administer opiates before their wounds were dressed.

A. That afternoon I think I mentioned that I gave them opiates about 2 hours after they were wounded, and that night I went to see them again and administered opiates and it was my custom after that each morning before they started to give them an opiate, and to see them during the day as the column moved along, and always at night I did that.

Q. Did you examine their wounds at any time between the time they were wounded until their wounds were dressed.

A. Yes sir, I examined their wounds that same afternoon.

Q. How soon after they were wounded.

A. In about 2 hours I think. I got into the wagon and rode with them some distance. I used to direct the wagon to the right or left of the column to find smooth ground.

Q. Did the wagon keep up.

A. Not immediately. Every night it would come in. Often it would be several miles behind. I ordered the driver to go according to the feeling of the men, and it would be some distance behind, but it would come in every evening.

Q. Did that occur till the command got to Fort Wallace.

A. Yes sir.

Q. Do you know how far it is from the point where those men were wounded to Fort Wallace.

A. I think from Riverside Station to Fort Wallace is about 200 miles, and that was a few hours march after we left the Platte. I should say it was 180 or 190 miles those men were carried after they were wounded.

Questions by the Accused

Q. Did you understand or construe any remark or order given by the accused from the time you first saw the deserters till after they passed out of your charge to be an order not to render them medical attendance.

A. No sir.

Q. When you reached camp on the night of the 7th and gave the deserters medical attendance who directed you or instructed you to give them that attendance.

A. Gen. Custer.

Q. In what words or language did he give the order.

A. As far as I recollect now he said to me, "Doctor my sympathies are not with these men who are wounded, but I want you to give them all necessary attention."

Q. Did he or not direct you to report to him after you made an examination that night.

A. He did.

Q. Did you so report.

A. I did.

Q. What was the condition of those men as reported to him.

A. I gave an exact history to him of their wounds and how they were getting along.

Q. Did you have full control of those deserters, and were you allowed every authority to attend to them, the same as other patients.

A. Yes sir.

Q. Did or did not the accused frequently inquire after their condition.

A. Yes sir, always at night he inquired and sometimes during the march.

Q. Before dressing the wounds of those deserters did you or did you not state to the accused that the blood drying on the wounds would be the best that could be done for them.

A. I did. I spoke to several officers and tried to explain to them that that was the best I could do for them.

Q. Was or was not the wagon conveying those deserters under your charge during the march.

A. It was entirely. I commanded the wagon.

Q. Did you or did you not ask the accused to keep that wagon for those men, to save the trouble of loading and unloading them, when they would be disturbed.

A. I did.

Q. How did the injuries of Johnson compare with the injuries of the other men.

A. His injuries were more severe. The others received merely flesh wounds.

Q. Did you consider any of those men to be mortally wounded at that time.

A. I did not at that time.

Q. Did you or did you not so report to the accused.

A. I did, and I thought they were not and I would explain that Johnson, who afterwards died, was the most cheerful at that time.

Q. State whether in your opinion the man Johnson did or did not die in consequence of any order given by the accused in regard to medical attendance.

A. He did not.

Q. In the case of a man wounded more than once, could not one shot have produced all wounds, or could two shots have produced three wounds; that is, was each one of the wounds produced by different shots.

A. In those cases I think each wound except in the case of Johnson was produced by different shots; that was my opinion at the time.

Q. In regard to the use of the ambulance, did you have occasion to put other patients in a wagon in preference to the ambulance.

A. I have since that.

Questions by the Court

Q. If the person who shot Johnson in the head had been 20 or 25 yards from him at the time, would or would not the shot have went directly through his head without passing down into his lungs.

A. A shot at that distance might have taken the exact course it did. A very slight thing will turn the course of a ball. If you will allow me, it is recorded in medical history of a ball having struck the breast bone, and to have been found lodged in the testicles. I know of one instance of a ball striking what is known as the "Adams Apple" and passing clear around the neck and was taken out at the very same place.

Q. Did the wagon in which the wounded men were brought to Fort Wallace, arrive at that post at the same time with the command.

A. It arrived there at the time or immediately after. We arrived there in the evening and the wagon also arrived there that evening; it was perhaps a mile or two behind the column.

Question by a Member

Q. What did you understand the accused to mean when he directed you not to go near the wagon containing the wounded men when they first came in, and why did you not attend to them immediately when they were brought in.

The question was objected to by the Judge Advocate, as he was apprehensive the answer might not be of any benefit to the prosecution.

The Court was cleared for deliberation and upon re-opening the doors it was announced that the Judge Advocate withdrew his objection.

A. I had at that time an idea the objection was made for effect. There had been a great many desertions some 30 or 40 the night previous, and the men were crowding around the wagon and I had an idea the General wished to make an impression on the men that they would be dealt with in the severest and harshest manner. I stood back as soon as he gave the order. Soon after the column started and the men were in their proper places, as I said before, I attended to the men.

Q. When you attended to the wounded men 2 hours after they were brought in, as you have stated, did you do so by order of Gen. Custer or in disobedience of his orders.

A. Soon after I had started to those men, I think just before Gen. Custer moved out with the column or it might have been immediately after he told me not to go near them; he said "you can attend to them after a while." or "It will be time enough to attend to them after a while" or some such expression as that. He said that to me.

Q. Why did you not attend to those wounded men until after the expiration of 2 hours after they were brought in.

A. It was 2 hours after they were wounded. At least one hour expired after they were wounded till they got into camp and about half an hour was expended in getting under way, and I did not attend to them until after the column got under way. The order given not to go near those men was about an hour after they were wounded, and it was perhaps a half hour or an hour before I got to see them after that. I waited until after the column moved out.

Q. Did you finally attend to the wounded men of your own accord, or was it by order of the accused.

A. By order of the accused. I received that expression as an order when he said it will be time enough to attend to them after a while or you can attend to those men after a while or some such expression. That was the only order I had at that time.

The witness having heard his testimony read over then retired.

The Judge Advocate announced that further and material witnesses for the prosecution were not yet in attendance although summoned in sufficient time; and asked the Court to adjourn.

At 12 P.M. the Court adjourned until 10:00 A.M. Sept. 27, 1867.

When the court convened the next day, the judge advocate announced that key witnesses for whom the Court had been waiting had not yet arrived and no one knew where they were. He then had Custer's official report about the march from the Platte to Fort Wallace and from Fort Wallace to Fort Riley read to the Court. Custer described the shooting of the deserters, and said he regretted their wounds had not been more serious. He mentioned again the men who were left behind near Downer's Station, saying that they had been sent back to pick up a man who had halted at the last ranch but avoids saying that the man had stopped to take care of Custer's mare. This version of the story is quite different from saying, as he did later, that the men had halted "without authority."

In his report, Custer gave an impassioned, but not entirely convincing, explanation for the grueling march from the Platte to Fort Wallace, blaming many of his problems, including some of the desertions, on the commissary department. "The march from the Platte to Fort Wallace was a forced one, from the fact that although my train contained rations for my command up to the 20th of the month yet when the stores came to be issued they were discovered to be in such a damaged condition that it would be with difficulty they could be made to last until we should reach Fort Wallace. And I take this opportunity to express the belief, a belief in which I am supported by facts as well as by the opinions of the officers associated under me, that the gross neglect and mismanagement exhibited in the Commissary Department through this District has subjected both officers and men to privations for which there was no occasion and which were never contemplated or intended by the Government when my command left Fort Hays for the Platte.

"The officers were only able to obtain hard bread and bacon, coffee and sugar for their private messes although it had been known weeks, if not months, before that a large command was expected to arrive at Fort Hays; in the same manner

it was known that an expedition was contemplated to the Platte. On my return march to Fort Wallace all hard bread not damaged was required to subsist the enlisted men, while the officers were actually compelled to pick up and collect from that portion of the hard bread which had been condemned and abandoned, a sufficient amount to subsist themselves to Fort Wallace. That this bread was damaged will not appear remarkable when it is known that some of the boxes were marked 1860."

The Court did not take testimony for the next several days because some witnesses were still missing and because General Custer was ill. When testimony did resume, several officers challenged statements made during Isaac Coates's testimony as witness for the prosecution. Major Joel Elliott, the first witness on the stand when the Court convened several days later, described the shooting of the deserters and their wagon trip back to camp. Under questioning, he said that although there was no surface water, it would have been possible to find "passably" clear water by digging. He repeated a conversation with Isaac Coates in which he had asked the doctor why he had not dressed the wounds of the wounded men and Isaac had replied that he had been ordered not to attend to their wounds.

Lieutenant Henry Jackson testified that he was within 150 yards of the wagon for almost the entire march but did not see Isaac Coates go near it. He also said that water was available six to eight inches below the surface of the sand. He thought that the men had received medical attention sometime during the night.

On October 7, Isaac Coates was recalled to testify, this time for the defense.

Questions by the Accused

Q. Did you state in your evidence for the prosecution that between the noon halt where those wounded deserters were brought in and the night camp of the 7th of July, you visited the wagon containing those wounded deserters.

A. Yes sir.

Q. State how soon that was after the column got under.

A. About half an hour.

Q. Did you administer any opiates to them at that time.

A. Yes sir.

Q. When the accused gave you, after arriving in camp, the order to give those deserters all necessary care did he give you any other instructions? if so what.

A. Yes sir, he told me not to say anything about that order he gave me, to the company commanders, because if they knew it, through them the men would get to know it.

Q. What order do you refer to.

A. That I was to give treatment to those wounded men.

Q. State why those instructions were given to you, as far as you know.

A. Because he did not wish the troops generally to know I was treating those men who were shot.

The witness having heard his testimony read over then retired.

In a long and eloquent written defense read by Custer's counsel, Brevet Lieutenant Colonel Charles Parsons, Custer pled for a finding of not guilty on all counts except for one, for which he asked for a decision of guilty but "attach no criminality there to." Toward the end of his testimony, he referred to the matter of the water. "There is some testimony in regard to the condition of the water at the camp of July seventh from Lt. Jackson which I suppose is intended to rebut Dr. Coates' views in regard to the propriety of dressing those men's wounds. I do not know anything about this. I am not on trial for malpractice, nor am I to be held responsible for Dr. Coates' professional views, although I will aver that from long observation I have the highest confidence in them. Hence it is sufficient to know that I did not stand in the way of the dressing of the wounds."

The court found General Custer guilty of all charges and specifications, except for the specification that Custer had refused to allow the surgeon to treat the wounded men. On this one issue, the court removed the harshest language and attached no criminality to the finding of guilty. General Custer was suspended from command and had to forfeit his pay for one year.

TWELVE

Isaac Coates
Leaves the Army

FOR REASONS NOT GIVEN in the records, Isaac Coates did not return to the Seventh Cavalry after his participation in the court-martial. The summary of his army contract now in the National Archives indicates that he was enroute from Fort Leavenworth to Fort McRae, New Mexico, with Company H of the Thirty-Eighth Infantry on October 10, just three days after his last testimony at the trial and one day before the court adjourned. It may be that nothing more sinister happened than a sudden opening for a post surgeon at Fort McRae, but it is also possible that Isaac was punished for testifying against Custer. It is clear that General Sheridan was sympathetic to Custer, and, as the newly appointed commander of the Department of the Missouri, was in a position to make his disapproval felt by those he might have thought guilty of unkindness to his friend Custer. Ironically, Isaac Coates's testimony was the only mitigating factor in an otherwise sweeping finding of guilty on all charges. On December 31, 1867, Isaac Coates reported to General Barnes that he was on duty as post surgeon at Fort McRae.[1]

While at Fort McRae, Isaac Coates received a letter from a lawyer in Frankfort, Kentucky, representing the family of Major Wickcliffe Cooper, the alcoholic officer who had committed suicide in June 1867. Cooper's widow asked for help in obtaining the survivor's pension, which the army refused to pay because the death certificate, signed by Isaac Coates, said the cause of death was suicide. Isaac subsequently became enmeshed in a bizarre sequence of events, which began when he naively responded to the lawyer's letter by sending him a signed, blank pension form, a violation of army regulations. In his letter of February 1 that accompanied the blank certificate, he asked the lawyer to be careful in how he filled out the form, noting that the army would make "the most serious charges" against him if there was any conflict between the pension request and the certificate he had completed at the time of the suicide. He added that he would consider it a pleasure and a duty to help Mrs. Cooper any way he could.

Isaac was rewarded for his kindness—and indiscretion—by a particularly nasty and inexplicable betrayal of trust on the part of the lawyer, who immediately passed along to the army the forms as well as Isaac's confidential letter. The army proceeded to annul his contract, but Isaac did not know it. Some time in late February or early March, Isaac resigned from the army to go home and settle an estate "worth some thousands of dollars." His friend and superior, Brevet Lieutenant Colonel J. Cooper McKee, chief medical officer, District of New Mexico, had been "very willing under the circumstances" to let Isaac resign. He also sent Isaac his "kind wishes and congratulations." Colonel McKee's letter to Isaac was dated March 4. Isaac wrote General Barnes on the fifteenth that he was "on this day relieved of duty." A few weeks later, Colonel McKee received instructions, obviously written before Isaac Coates's letter arrived in Washington, to annul Isaac's contract as soon as possible. McKee wrote back on April 7, possibly with a smirk, that Dr. Coates's contract had already been annulled on March 23 "at his own request" and that Isaac had "left for the States via San Francisco, Cal." Isaac Coates never received copies of any of the correspondence relating to his involuntary dismissal and was totally unaware of it until a year later.

On April 21, 1869, Isaac Coates wrote a letter to General Barnes applying for "a situation in the medical department of the army."[2] He was stunned when, three days later, he received a reply from the surgeon general's office: "Your request cannot be complied with, as your name had been placed on the list of Physicians not to be contracted with again, for the reason of having signed *Blank* Certificate for Pension in the case of the late Maj. Cooper." Isaac replied with an outraged letter to General Barnes expressing his profound "pain and mortification" that an act of his was being "looked upon with suspicion," citing as character references the names of most or all of the senior medical officers of the United States Cavalry and saying that, if he had done something wrong, it was through ignorance, not intent. His explanation for his ignorance—that he had never read a page of the army regulations—was probably not persuasive to a career army officer.

With the end of his military career, Isaac Coates returned to Chester, Pennsylvania.

THIRTEEN

Indian Wars of 1868

THE FIRST HALF of 1868 was relatively peaceful, but in August a Cheyenne war party raided homes and ranches on the Saline and Solomon rivers, killing men, women, and children. The Indians were well equipped for their work, since Agent Wynkoop had just issued them government rifles, pistols, and ammunition. The cavalry went after the Indians, but was unable to chase them down. A major loss to the army was the death of Bill Comstock, who was ambushed and killed by Cheyennes whom he had thought were friendly.

By September, the Union Pacific had reached Sheridan, Kansas, where its progress was stalled until more money could be found to keep the company going. Stagecoaches ran from the end of the rails to Denver, but continued Indian attacks on the Platte road and the Smoky Hill road were making travel dangerous. Phil Sheridan's solution was to organize a command of volunteer scouts under the leadership of Brevet Colonel George Forsythe. Forsythe recruited fifty experienced plainsmen, each man paid one dollar a day and thirty-five cents for use of his horse.

When news was received at Fort Wallace that a Mexican freight train on its way from Sheridan to Santa Fe had been attacked and men had been killed, Forsythe was ordered to pursue the war party. He caught up with the Indians on the Arikaree Fork of the Republican River. In what is now called the Beecher Island Fight, Colonel Forsythe's fifty scouts ran into hundreds more Indians than they could handle, led by Bull Bear, Tall

Bull, and White Horse. The fight went on for nine days, until Forsythe and his men were relieved by cavalry from Fort Wallace. Forsythe's losses were fifteen wounded and six killed, including Lieutenant Fred Beecher and the command surgeon, Dr. Mooers. The Indians' losses are unknown, but as they had charged many times into the repeating Spencer carbines and controlled fire of the scouts, their casualties could have been substantial. Perhaps the worst loss for the Indians was the death of Roman Nose, the great Cheyenne Dog Soldier war leader.

The Treaty of Medicine Lodge had not held through 1868. Indian raids and futile army retaliatory expeditions continued into the fall. In the same month as the Beecher Island Fight, Brevet Brigadier General Alfred Sully led a punitive expedition south from Fort Dodge but was unable to find any Indians to punish. By this time, a distinct change in the tone and content of military communications was evident, due partly to the arrival of General Hancock's replacement, General Sheridan, and also to General Sherman's utter frustration. In Kansas alone, 157 civilians were killed in the second half of 1868, many of them railroad construction workers. The goal of persuading the Indians to behave had given way to punishing the hostiles, with much less concern about which Indians were actually hostile and which were not.

On September 23, Sherman wrote his brother John: "The Indian war on the plains need simply amount to this. We have now selected and provided reservations for all, off the great roads. All who cling to their old hunting grounds are hostile and will remain so till killed off. We will have a sort of predatory war for years, every now and then be shocked by the indiscriminate murder of travellers and settlers, but the country is so large, and the advantage of the Indians so great, that we cannot make a single war and end it."[1]

Sherman also included a paragraph that is omitted from *The Sherman Letters*: "The more we can kill this year, the less will have to be killed the next war, for the more I see of these Indians the more convinced I am that they will all have to be killed or be maintained as a species of paupers. Their attempts at civilization are simply ridiculous."[2]

While Sherman and Sheridan were working out a strategy to catch the Indians in their winter camps, the Custers had moved to Monroe, Michigan, to wait out the general's exile. Meanwhile, Sherman and Sheridan lacked a cavalry commander who could be counted on to take troops into battle with reckless bravado. On September 23, a miltary telegram arrived in the adjutant general's office in Washington from General Sherman, asking that Custer be restored to duty immediately. On the twenty-fourth, Custer received a welcoming telegram from Sheridan. Delighted with the turn of events, Custer left immediately for the West, assuming field command of the campaign at Fort Dodge early in October.

On November 15, Thomas Murphy, superintendent of Indian Affairs, wrote from Topeka to N. G. Taylor, commissioner of the Office of Indian Affairs in Washington, that agents Wynkoop and Boone were out in Indian country with orders to congregate the Indians in the vicinity of Fort Cobb and expressing his alarm that a "large army" was marching in the same direction. On the twenty-first, Taylor wrote to the secretary of the interior with the same concerns. On November 29, not knowing that it was already too late, Wynkoop wrote Taylor to protest that five separate army columns were converging on the Washita, the place where he had persuaded the Indians to gather. Saying that he would not be "an instrument of the murder of innocent women and children," he resigned his commission.

Custer's victory at the Battle of the Washita, November 27, 1868, was not only a personal triumph but also confirmation of Sherman and Sheridan's decision to recall him from exile and validation of Sheridan's strategy to go after the Indians when they were in winter camp. Sheridan immediately issued extravagant declarations of praise for the Seventh Cavalry. Custer claimed 103 Cheyenne men killed and 53 women and children taken prisoner. He did not mention dead women and children. Other sources suggested fewer than 20 men and up to 40 women and children were killed. Army losses included Major Elliott, Captain Hamilton, and 19 enlisted men killed; Captain Barnitz, lieutenants Custer and March, and 11 enlisted men wounded. Custer's men shot 800 Indian horses and captured large quantities of clothing and equipment essential to the Indians' survival in the winter.

After the fight, Custer happily reported that Black Kettle's scalp was in the possession of one of the Osage scouts. Black Kettle was described by George Bird Grinnell as "a striking example of a consistently friendly Indian, who, because he was friendly and so because his whereabouts was usually known, was punished for the acts of people whom it was supposed he could control."[3]

Custer's victory at the Washita was a devastating defeat for the Indians, one from which they never really recovered. Fighting on the southern plains continued for almost another decade, but it soon became a vengeful, hopeless lashing out by Indians at white people. It is interesting to speculate whether the winter campaign of 1868 would have been handled differently, and less effectively, by other commanders. Would Hancock, for example, have taken Lone Wolf and Satanta hostage for the compliance of their people, and then begun proceedings to hang them, as Sheridan did? If so, he probably would have received Sherman's support if he had hanged them, since Sherman had said that he wanted Satanta and Bull Bear killed before any negotiations could take place. By the fall of 1868, sixteen months after Hancock hesitated before burning the village on the Pawnee Fork, the army high command was issuing official communications that included phrases such as "go ahead, kill and punish [the Indians]," and the government is "the source of all authority" not "a few thieving, treacherous chiefs of predatory bands of savages." Cruel as it seemed to Isaac Coates, the expedition of 1867 appears almost naive compared to the harsh official policy that evolved after "Hancock's War."

FOURTEEN

Isaac Coates:
His Last Fifteen Years

WITH THE TERMINATION of Isaac Coates's military service and therefore his obligation to file monthly reports to General Barnes, he lost the security of his $100-per-month salary and we lost a reliable, orderly chronicle of the course of his life. Although these reports were very concise—in fact they usually said just enough to prove that he was on duty—they nonetheless did include a date and place. And we know from other sources that entries such as "In the field on the South Fork of the Republican River" meant that Isaac was in the thick of things, living through events of dramatic intensity and great historic interest. The last fifteen years of his life, from 1868 to 1883, were, if anything, more crammed with adventure than his spring and summer on the plains, but, regrettably, we have only fragments of the story—a few letters, brief mention of him in the files of some of the organizations to which he belonged, photographs, some public records, newspaper articles, and one short journal written for his son, Harold.

From Fort McRae, Isaac somehow made his way to San Francisco and then home to Chester, either crossing the entire country by stagecoach and horseback, or by traveling by ship down the coast of California to Central America, across the Isthmus of Panama, and up the East Coast of the United States to New York or Philadelphia. Fifteen years and many thousands of miles later, he would finish his life in Socorro, New Mexico, just seventy miles north of Fort McRae.

We do not know exactly when Isaac reached home, but we know it was in time to nurse his then-only child, Pierre, in the last months of his life before he died of consumption, at the age of two years and eleven months. Isaac practiced medicine in Chester for the next several years, having failed in his 1869 attempt to obtain another position with the army. In June 1870, Harold (my wife's grandfather) was born, and then Charles was born in 1871, but he died at birth. In the latter part of 1871, wanderlust, or perhaps inadequate financial resources, or, possibly, an unhappy life at home persuaded Isaac to go adventuring again, this time to Peru as medical director of the Chimbote and Huaraz Railway. His employer, Henry Meiggs, described as "redoubtable" by contemporary newspapers, had left California in a hurry after making and losing a fortune and being accused of forgery. He began his South American railroad-building career in Chile, then moved to Peru, where he succeeded in building the Chimbote and Huaraz. He next undertook the nearly impossible task of driving a railroad over the Andes, from the seaport of Callao to the mines of the La Oroya district, crossing the mountains at an elevation of 15,800 feet. He almost succeeded but ran out of money in 1875 before completing the project. Financially ruined, he retired to Lima, where he died in 1877.

Even though the Callao to La Oroya line was a financial disaster for Meiggs, his South American railroad ventures were extraordinary feats of engineering and construction. His Callao railroad became the Central Railway, one of four railroads transporting ore from the mines and refineries high up in the Andes to ports along the coast. The Central is the highest standard gauge railroad in the world. Isaac Coates, as medical director of the Chimbote and Huaraz, was on the ground with the construction crews, and he shared the hardships of working in a climate and over terrain that is thought to have been far worse than the conditions faced by construction crews in the western United States.

We have a small photograph of an officer in full-dress naval uniform inscribed, "In token of sincere regard to Dr. Coates from his faithful friend

Honorado G. Firon, Peruvian Navy, Chimbote, Mayo 23, 1872." At that time, before the construction of the railroad to the mines, Chimbote was a small seacoast village. It is now a city of 278,000.

From the photograph of Senor Firon, we know where Isaac was in May 1872, but we have no clues as to how he spent the next fifteen months. As it is unlikely that he left Peru, he probably continued to perform his duties with the railroad for most of that time. In his history of the army medical department, P. M. Ashburn says that Isaac Coates studied earthquakes in South America for the Smithsonian Institution during 1872 and 1873, recording thirty-six, which may explain why he emerges again from the shadows seven hundred miles south of Chimbote near the town of Arequipa. Arequipa had been leveled by a major earthquake in 1868, and it is possible that Isaac made his way down to southern Peru hunting earthquakes. We do know that on September 23, 1873, Isaac Coates made the first recorded ascent of the volcano El Misti, or Mount Arequipa, which Isaac thought was 18,600 feet in elevation but is actually 19,101 feet high. We have the tiny American flag he carried to the summit, the highest known point to which the American flag had been carried up to that time.

After his triumphant ascent of the volcano, Isaac may have rejoined Henry Meiggs before Meiggs was forced by lack of money to terminate his part in the construction of the Callao, Lima, and La Oroya railroad. Or he may have gone on climbing mountains or even became involved in some other project, possibly archaeology. Although there is no mention anywhere in his papers of participation in an archaeological dig, and the organizations to which he belonged cannot find any record of a trip to Peru at that time, his files contain photographs of skulls, skeletons, and even a complete mummy. Some of the pictures had been taken by a Lima photographer, but others were made in Chester, which suggests that the bones were in his possession after he returned to the United States. We also have a small, gold effigy that could have come from an excavated Inca grave. It is likely, therefore, that Isaac had more than a casual connection with an archaeological project somewhere in Peru.

In a letter from Chester dated May 27, 1879, to the American Geographical Society, of which he was a fellow, Isaac Coates mentions letters
he published in the *South Pacific Times* of Callao describing a journey he
made across the South American continent during October, November,
and December 1875. He began at Pacasmayo, on the west coast of Peru,
350 miles north of Lima, and traversed the Andes of northern Peru, passing through Cajamarca, Chachapoyas, Mayabamba, and Tarapoto to
Chasuta. From Chasuta, he took a canoe 150 miles down the Huallaga
River to Yurimaguas, where he changed to a raft and continued on for 600
miles to Iquitos. For some unexplained reason, he was detained in Iquitos
but was finally able to hire a Peruvian steam launch for a trip up the Rio
Napo. He says in his letter that he was the first person to navigate the Rio
Napo by steamer. After that adventure, Isaac boarded a commercial
steamer and descended the Amazon for 2,800 miles to Para, on the east
coast of Brazil, and then sailed for home.

By the time he returned to Chester in the spring of 1876, Isaac Coates's
travels in South America and his service with the Hancock expedition
against the Indians had earned him the status of distinguished citizen in
his home town. On May 25, he was asked by the centennial committee of
the citizens of Chester to deliver the Fourth of July Centennial Oration,
an honor he took very seriously indeed. With slightly more than a month
to prepare it, Isaac produced an address replete with remarkably detailed
information about the economic development of the United States, by
each year from 1790 to 1840, summarizing production statistics for industry and agriculture and adding brief notes for each year about events
he thought especially interesting. Some samples follow:

> 1790. Ship Columbia, of Boston, completed first American voyage around
> the world.
>
> 1792. A mint was established in Philadelphia. The power first used for
> coining was by four or five horses.
>
> 1796. First successful manufacture of sugar from the cane in Louisiana, by
> M. E. Bore, who sold his crop at $12,000, then considered a large sum.

1840. In England it takes sixty females to stick in one day, by sunlight, ninety packs consisting of 302,460 pins. The same operation is performed near Derby, Connecticut, by one woman in the same time.

Entries of this kind were made for every year up to 1841. He also summarized the decades 1841–50 and 1851–60, giving manufacturing and demographic statistics. He then continued with more detailed information about years 1870 to 1875.

The oration was subsequently published by J. B. Lippincott & Co. in a handsome, leather-bound volume of sixty-four pages, the first forty of which were devoted to statistics and observations about various activities, ranging from newspapers to illuminating gas to missionaries. The balance of the speech, a collection of philosophical observations about a range of subjects, tells us a great deal about Isaac Coates, the man. He was then forty-two years old and admired for his erudition and his adventurous life, which he describes as "somewhat checkered." He was confident and willing to express his convictions, in sometimes passionate terms, about issues of the day. Apparently, he was in good health at the time, not yet troubled by rheumatic fever, which was probably the cause of his death six years later.

Typical of Isaac's love of literary and classical references, the published version of the oration begins with quotations from Milton, Addison, Plato, and the Temple of Minerva. Isaac apparently believed and felt deeply what Plato had expressed millennia ago: "Could we create so close, tender, and cordial a connection between the citizens of a State as to induce all to consider themselves as relatives—as fathers, brothers, and sisters—then this whole State would constitute but a single family, be subjected to the most perfected regulations, and become the happiest republic that ever existed upon the earth."

After the statistical analysis of the country's economic history, Isaac divided his speech into separate themes, with titles such as "Wisdom of the Fathers," in which he discussed the genius of the founding fathers in realizing that man has the capacity for self-government if he combines humanity with common sense. His dissertation on the importance of compulsory, universal education urges that "every dirty, ragged child of every beggar and felon in the land" be compelled to receive "a gratuitous education." He reserves his most forceful arguments for the subject of religion in government, "this mischievous, cruel, envious, ambitious, sanguinary, rule-or-ruin hideous monster. ... This ambition of religion for universal supremacy, for absolute power, is dangerous. No danger could be more threatening to our national existence than the unity of church and state."

The last paragraph of the speech, which may have been talked about for years afterward, is as follows:

> When, a few years hence, a more generous, ennobling, and enlightened spirit of humanity shall have completely annihilated a detestable species of selfishness abroad in our land; when we, as American citizens—enjoying all the rights and privileges of man—shall be brought to feel and acknowledge that down-trodden and oppressed foreigners, from whatever quarter of the globe, have as good a right to seek protection and a home on the soil of America as our forefathers had, who were themselves but downtrodden and oppressed foreigners; and when America shall be not only an asylum for the oppressed of all other nations, but a kind and impartial mother to all her own children; when patriotism and philanthropy shall join hands; when over the threshold of the great temple of American liberty there shall be engraved, as the law of the land, plain and eternal as if written with the golden point of Orion's sword, on the ebon walls of night, these words: EQUAL AND EXACT JUSTICE TO ALL, WITHOUT REGARD TO RELIGION, NATIONALITY, COLOR, OR SEX; then, indeed, shall our great country be elevated to the most exalted and sublime eminence among the nations of the earth.

On June 25, 1876, Isaac Coates sat in his living room in Chester, putting the finishing touches on his Centennial Oration. Two thousand miles away to the west, his old comrades of the Seventh Cavalry rode to the top of a hill above the Little Bighorn River and looked down on a vast encampment of Sioux and Cheyennes. A few hours later, Isaac's friends—George Armstrong Custer, Tom Custer, William Cooke, Myles Keogh, and George Yates—were dead, lying scattered across the rolling prairie. Isaac did not hear the news until after the Fourth of July.

In August 1877, Mary Penn-Gaskell Coates, whom Isaac Coates never mentions in his journals and whom he saw only occasionally during their twenty-two years of married life, died at her parents' home in Philadelphia.

Six months later, in February 1878, Isaac Coates returned to Brazil as surgeon on the Collins Expedition to Brazil and Bolivia. He took with him his seven-year-old son, Harold, on what developed into a disastrous undertaking. Philip and Thomas Collins of Philadelphia held a contract with the Madeira and Mamore Railway Company and the National Bolivian Navigation Company to construct "a Railway and other works on the banks of the River Madeira [a tributary of the Amazon] within the Empire of Brazil ... from a point on the bank of the River Madeira at or near San Antonio to a point on the River Mamore in the vicinity of Guajara Merim." Many of the members of the expedition ended up dying of tropical fever and, possibly, starvation.

Isaac Coates wrote a brief, touching account of his and Harold's harrowing experiences, in which both were lucky to have survived the miserable living conditions, hunger, injuries, and illness. The story is full of affection and pride for the little boy's courage. On July 7, 1878, they ran "Dos Marrinhas" rapids on the Madeira River in a canoe paddled by ten Indians, all shouting at once because "they had conflicting views about the channel." The canoe filled with water and almost capsized but remained upright until they could reach shore. Isaac Coates was seriously ill with "rheumatism" on the voyage down to Brazil and on the expedition up the Amazon.

In May 1879, Isaac wrote the American Geographical Society from Chester asking if the society would be interested in some letters he had written about his trip across South America in 1875. He also offered to give a one-hour talk "with or without stereoptican," assuring the society that he would try not to be boring. He mentioned that he planned to go to Colorado in a week or two.

He wrote again in January, acknowledging receipt of a letter from the society asking for his letters. The society's letter, written by Robert Curren, Esq., chief clerk, must have reached Isaac some months earlier because he apologizes for the "long silence" and explains he had been "dangerously ill of a rheumatic fever." He had left Colorado in December when he was well enough to travel again. Isaac asks the society to reimburse him for his expenses, which he says were double what they should have been "owing to our losses and the animals we bought."

In 1881, Isaac Coates returned to Colorado, perhaps just on a visit or, perhaps, to practice medicine. In August, a poem by Dr. Isaac Taylor Coates entitled "That Our Good President May Not Die" was published in Pueblo, Colorado. The poem was an ode to President James Garfield, who had been shot on July 2 and died on September 19. From Pueblo, Isaac Coates went south to Socorro, New Mexico, where he practiced medicine in partnership with a Doctor Sherman.

On June 23, 1883, Isaac's son, Harold, was visiting friends at a ranch outside of Socorro, when a messenger arrived from town with the news that Isaac had died. Isaac's brother, Joseph, made the necessary arrangements by telegraph from Pennsylvania, and in due course, the thirteen-year-old boy accompanied his father's casket back home to Chester. Harold then went to live with Isaac's sister, Annie, and her husband, Charles Morton. Isaac Coates lies with his mother and his stillborn baby in the Chester Rural Cemetery.

Notes

Introduction

1. R. David Edmunds, *American Indian Leaders*, 109.
2. Captain Eugene F. Ware, *The Indian War of 1864*, 147.
3. Rachel Sherman Thorndike, *The Sherman Letters*, 277.
4. Ibid., 287.
5. Ibid., 289.
6. Difficulties with Indian Tribes. 41st Cong., 2 sess., H.R. Exec. Doc. No. 240, 98, 99.
7. Ibid., 13.
8. Ibid., 28.
9. *Personal Memoirs of U.S. Grant*, 539, 540.
10. Henry M. Stanley, *My Early Travels and Adventures in America*, xvi.
11. Document #240, 93, 94.

Chapter One

1. Washington Irving (1783–1859), historian, biographer, essayist, diplomat, and explorer, was one of the preeminent American literary figures of the first half of the nineteenth century. The books that inspired Isaac Coates to go looking for Indians in 1867 were written in the mid-1830s, twenty-five years after Irving wrote his enormously popular spoof of the old New York Dutch burgher-aristocracy, *A History of New York from the Beginning of the World to the End of the Dutch Dynasty*. In 1832, Irving embarked on a journey down the Ohio and west to St. Louis, and then up the Arkansas to the Cimarron. He hunted buffalo and studied the Indians who lived in the area. Although Irving was only out for a month, he returned home with enough notes and observations to write *Tour of the Prairies*, certainly one of the books Isaac read and treasured. Isaac would have seen in Irving's writings his admiration and affection for the Indians he met on the trip. Two other books that may well have been in Isaac's library were Irving's *Astoria* and *The Adventures of Captain Bonneville*, both stories of the fur trade in

the far west. Irving condemned the cruel treatment of west coast Indians by the fur traders.

2. Morpheus, in Greek and Roman mythology, was the god of dreams. Lethe was the river of forgetfulness in the Hades of Greek mythology.

3. Edward Young (1683–1765), "Night Thoughts."

4. A Greek painter who lived about 400 B.C.

5. Isaac refers here to a certain lack of enthusiasm for progress and industry, other than agriculture, which characterized Mormon leadership of the time.

6. Scott was probably Thomas Alexander Scott who was first vice-president and, later, president of the Pennsylvania Railroad and was credited with its rapid expansion after the Civil War. Felton is not so easy to identify, but Isaac may possibly have been referring to William Harrell Felton, who was a member of Congress from Georgia and led efforts to assure the financial soundness of American railroads.

7. Perhaps Lincoln scholars will readily recognize this paean to the murdered president, but I was unable to find it anywhere.

8. What Isaac Coates calls "the age of bridges and the train," others have named the time of "railroad fever." From the mid-1830s almost to the end of the century, investors, speculators, builders, and talented scoundrels enthusiastically promoted the construction of railroads and the formation of railroad companies throughout the United States. Isaac was riding on the Pennsylvania, a railroad that, for the most part, escaped the skullduggery that plagued so many other lines because it was built on solid financial footing from the beginning, and had a genius, John Edgar Thomson, as its chief engineer. Isaac could ride on a single train from Philadelphia to Pittsburgh, and on to Chicago, because Thomson, only a decade or so before, had put together a consolidated system of small railroads and newly constructed track to form the main line across Pennsylvania and points west. The first passenger train had passed over the entire route from Philadelphia to Pittsburgh just nine years before Isaac's trip.

In paying tribute to the accomplishments of the American railroads, Isaac Coates does not distinguish between the successful roads and those that failed, losing millions of dollars for their investors. Nor does he acknowledge the dark side of railroad construction and financing at the time; the companies did not always benefit from the success of their own operations. Instead, individual officers and directors enriched themselves at the expense of the companies. At about the same time that Isaac was exulting in the glories of railroads and bridges, the New York and Erie Rail Road Company was being plundered by Daniel Drew, Jay Gould, and James Fisk. In December 1867, the Credit Mobilier scandal—involving kickbacks, inflated pricing, and bribery of congressional members—came to light, shocking the country and rocking the Union Pacific. Out in California, the Central Pacific was operating with its own share of scandalous construction contracts, while its directors were doing very well indeed. With so much publicly acknowledged corruption, it is surprising that Isaac did not slip in, however reluctantly, a cautionary note along with his description of railroads as the "great civilizers."

9. The Kansas-Pacific was also known as the Union Pacific, Eastern Division.

Chapter Two

1. With the signing of the Kansas-Nebraska Act of 1854 by President Pierce, Kansas Territory became a training ground for the Civil War. The act left it up to the settlers of the territory to decide whether Kansas would be slaveholding or free. Proslavery forces from Missouri flooded into Kansas and clashed with abolitionists dispatched from New England to keep the territory free. The elections of 1854 and 1855 were stolen by armed Missourians who set up a territorial government in Lecompton. The abolitionists established a rival government in Topeka. Shooting started in 1855 with the killing of a Free State man, and for the next several years, "Bleeding Kansas" was racked by open warfare. Men were shot down because they were thought to support one side or the other, and women and children were driven from their homes. In 1856, Lawrence was sacked by a mob of proslavery Southerners. John Brown and his fanatics retaliated by sabering to death five proslavery settlers. In 1858, proslavery forces herded eleven Free State men into a ravine, lined them up, and shot them. Kansas became a state in 1861 with a constitution that forbade slavery, but the hatreds of the previous five years remained and festered. When proslavery William Quantrill and his guerrillas invaded Lawrence from Missouri in 1863, their orders were to "kill every male and burn every house in Lawrence." Quantrill managed to kill 183 men and boys before pulling back into Missouri.

2. Edward Bulwer-Lytton (1803–1873), "Richelieu," 1839.

3. "Give the devil his due" apparently originated with Miguel de Cervantes (1547–1616) and comes from his *Don Quixote de la Mancha* (1605–1615).

4. The Hyperboreans of early Greek legend lived in blissful comfort in the far north, beyond the place where the North Wind begins.

5. Elizabeth Custer, *Tenting on the Plains*, 516.

6. The Santa Fe Trail was opened by Captain William Becknell in 1821 as a trade route from the Missouri River to the markets of New Mexico. The trail left the Missouri at Independence and headed west through Council Grove to Fort Zarah, where it joined the Arkansas River. Near Fort Larned, the trail split into two branches that came together again near Fort Dodge. West of Fort Dodge,

the traveler could choose between the Cimarron cutoff, which headed directly southwest to Fort Union, or the longer but easier mountain route, which continued along the Arkansas past Bent's Fort and Fort Lyon, and then turned south at a point west of the Purgatoire River. A stage system was established in 1850. Traffic along the trail reached prodigious proportions just before the Civil War. In 1860, for example, 3,033 wagons, 9,084 men, 6,147 mules and 27,920 oxen plodded along all or part of the 800 miles from the Missouri to Santa Fe.

The Fort Larned that Isaac saw in early 1867 was already recognized as one of the most important military posts on the western frontier, but it still looked a little shoddy. Some men still lived in dugouts along the banks of the Pawnee Fork. Although the old, dilapidated sod and adobe structures, some of them dating from 1859, were gradually being replaced by the handsome sandstone buildings that now line the parade ground, the enlisted men's barracks would not be finished until later in 1867. The officers' quarters, quartermaster storehouse, and shops building were completed early in 1868. Fort Larned guarded the Kansas part of the Santa Fe Trail. When, in 1865, Indian raids became a severe problem along the trail, Fort Larned served as the eastern end of an escort system for wagon trains that moved between there and Fort Union. From 1861 to 1868, Indian Bureau annuities of clothing and other goods were distributed to the Cheyennes, Arapahos, Kiowas, and Comanches at Fort Larned. Fort Larned was also the pivotal army post during the Indian battles of 1868 and 1869. It was abandoned in 1878 after finishing its final job, the protection of construction crews on the Santa Fe Railroad.

Chapter Three

1. Henry M. Stanley, *My Early Travels and Adventures in America*, 20.

2. Tall Bull and White Horse were chiefs of the Dog Soldier Society of southern Cheyennes, which included about one hundred lodges and five hundred people. The Dog Soldiers were one of six military societies among the Cheyennes. Although tribal government was traditionally in the hands of tribal chiefs of the Council of Forty-Four, the military societies gradually assumed more power as the war with the whites continued and Indian customs disintegrated. Military society leaders were "chosen to die" and were expected to embody courage and disregard for personal safety. The Dog Soldier Society was unique among Cheyenne societies because it had become a cohesive band within the tribe, led not by tribal chiefs but by war chiefs. The Dog Soldiers camped as a group, rather than scattered throughout the tribe. (See *The Cheyenne Way*, by Karl N. Llewellyn and E.

Adamson Hoebel for a thorough treatment of Cheyenne government and legal institutions.)

Tall Bull was one of the chiefs who signed the Medicine Lodge Treaty of 1867, but he continued to lead the dwindling Cheyenne forces in raids and fights in western Kansas and eastern Colorado. He was among the Indian leaders at the Battle of Beecher Island in September 1868. Tall Bull was shot and killed, with many of his Dog Soldier warriors, at the Battle of Summit Springs in July 1869.

White Horse continued the fight for the next five years, an extraordinary feat of courage since the Dog Soldier band had been reduced to mere remnants of its former power after Summit Springs. In the fall of 1869, he took some of his band north to the Wind River country to join the northern Cheyennes. White Horse later moved south, with other Cheyenne war parties, into the Texas Panhandle country. In 1874, convinced that more fighting would simply result in the death of all the surviving Cheyennes, White Horse surrendered his command—one old man, eleven warriors, and thirteen women.

3. Hancock called him "Geary." When Custer mentions him at all, Edmund Guerrier is simply the "half-breed" interpreter who was sent by Hancock to watch over the Indian village or to accompany Custer and Coates in their midnight search after the Indians had escaped. Custer says that Guerrier wanted to prevent bloodshed because he was married to a full-blooded Cheyenne woman who lived in the village. Both Custer and Hancock seemed to have been oblivious to Guerrier's essential role as shuttle-diplomat, interpreter, and peacemaker. Guerrier did not attract much attention, which was undoubtedly just the way he preferred it. He had already risked his life to carry messages between the white government and the Indians who, remarkably, continued to trust him and accept him as a friend even when he was interpreting and carrying messages for the army.

Guerrier was actually married to Julia Bent, daughter of the trader and Indian agent William Bent and definitely not a full-blooded Cheyenne. He frequently lived with the Cheyennes, however, and narrowly missed being killed when Colonel John Chivington attacked Black Kettle's village on Sand Creek. In the summer of 1864, Guerrier wrote a letter for the Cheyenne chiefs expressing their desire to make peace with the whites. Major Edward Wynkoop accepted their overtures as genuine and brought the chiefs to Denver for a conference with Governor Evans. Wynkoop wanted peace, but Chivington wanted war, and Chivington won. In their agony after Sand Creek, the Cheyennes could have blamed anyone who had had a part in the negotiations that led to the massacre, but they did not hold Guerrier responsible.

Hancock depended on Guerrier to translate his speeches to the Indian chiefs as well as their replies. In 1908, Guerrier told Grinnell that Hancock had threatened to hold him personally responsible if the Indian families left their village. Knowing the threat was absurd, Guerrier told Hancock that he would not go to the village on those terms. Hancock quickly relented and then asked Guerrier to go to the village and merely report if any Indians ran away. Guerrier rode to the village and talked at length with the Indian leaders, who told him openly of their fears and their plans to run away with the women and children. It is said that Guerrier delayed giving his report to Hancock until the Indians could get safely away. Guerrier then guided Custer on the forced march to the Smoky Hill in pursuit of the Indians.

Guerrier played an active role in other negotiations with the Cheyennes. In September 1867, he carried a letter to the Cheyenne chiefs inviting them to participate in the councils preceding the signing of the Medicine Lodge Treaty. A week later, he returned to Medicine Lodge with Roman Nose, Grey Beard, and other Cheyenne leaders. By 1877, the Cheyennes had been driven onto a reservation in what is now Oklahoma. By mid-summer of that year, the Northern Cheyennes, especially, were starving on government rations and dying of disease. Little Wolf talked with a government agent and told him that his people would all die if they did not return to the north country. He said he did not want to fight, but that they would have to leave. Guerrier subsequently went out to the Cheyenne camp and asked the leaders to come in and talk. He did the interpreting in the discussions that led to the last diaspora of the Cheyenne people. Finally, after all the years of being a trusted intermediary, Guerrier was warned by his Cheyenne relatives that he might be killed if he continued to interpret the conversations between the Indians and the government.

4. Hancock was referring to the murder and kidnapping of members of the Box family of Texas by Kiowas. The Cheyenne and Sioux chiefs probably had no idea what Hancock was talking about.

5. Isaac Coates first met Edward Wynkoop (1836–1891) when the expedition reached Fort Larned. Wynkoop was at the time the agent for the Cheyennes and Arapahos. At Hancock's request, Wynkoop had summoned the Cheyenne chiefs to a council at Fort Larned, the consequences of which Isaac describes in his journal. The chiefs came to Fort Larned because they considered Wynkoop to be their friend, a position of trust that Wynkoop had struggled for years to achieve. He had not always been the passionate defender of Indian interests that he was when Isaac watched him ride alone into the ranks of warriors confronting Hancock on the march to the village, and defuse a tense situation. Previously, in June and July 1863, Wynkoop had led units of the First Colorado Volunteers on a fruitless chase of Ute cattle thieves. And in August 1864, when commanding Fort Lyon, he had driven off attacking Indians, probably Kiowas, declaring he would kill every Indian he saw. Later in August, Wynkoop had led troops against a

greatly superior force of Cheyennes and Arapahos but escaped total annihilation through the intervention of Black Kettle and other chiefs. At about this time, Wynkoop had begun to change his mind about the morality of killing Indians and emerged some months later as a staunch supporter of Indian rights. In October 1864, believing that the chiefs really did want peace, he had made the terrible mistake of promising the chiefs protection and urging them to move to Sand Creek, thus exceeding his authority and inviting retaliation by Evans, Chivington, and the other Indian punishers. Wynkoop was subsequently relieved of his command and was therefore unable to provide the protection he had promised. The result was the Sand Creek massacre.

In June 1865, Wynkoop was appointed chief of cavalry for the District of the Upper Arkansas. In that capacity he was responsible for providing military escort to the peace commission that eventually produced the Treaty of the Little Arkansas. In arranging to bring the Cheyenne chiefs to the council Wynkoop found, to his amazement, that Black Kettle and his people knew all about Wynkoop's part in exposing the Indians to the Colorado Volunteers at Sand Creek but had no doubts about his good faith. In the fall of 1865, Wynkoop was appointed special agent for the Cheyennes and Arapahos, with the rank of brevet lieutenant colonel. Later he was appointed regular agent for the Cheyennes and Arapahos of the Upper Arkansas.

Wynkoop's efforts to develop a program for the Indians in which they were rewarded for good behavior and selectively punished for transgressions came to a halt with the arrival of General Hancock and his expedition. After that, Wynkoop suffered through one disaster after another—a village was burned, Indians were blamed for depredations he was convinced they did not do, and, finally, the Plains tribes resumed their raids in a general war of revenge. In the fall of 1868, Wynkoop knew that Sherman and Sheridan were preparing a winter campaign at the same time as the tribes were coming in closer to Fort Cobb for protection. Horrified at the prospect of another Sand Creek massacre, Wynkoop wrote a bitter letter of resignation to Commissioner of Indian Affairs N. G. Taylor on November 27. On November 28, Custer sent his troops into the Cheyenne village, which began the Battle of the Washita. For more about Wynkoop's life, read *The Tall Chief: The Autobiography of Edward W. Wynkoop*, edited by Christopher B. Gerboth.

6. Henry M. Stanley, *My Early Travels and Adventures in America*, 47.

Chapter Four

1. Pawnee Killer was one of the greatest of all the war chiefs of the Southern Oglala Sioux. In the summer of 1867, he circled the Seventh Cavalry on the march, striking when he could and talking when it served his purpose. He

harassed and outsmarted Custer. On June 24, the Sioux attacked Custer's camp, shot a sentry, and then met in council with Custer to talk the whole thing over. Later the same day, Pawnee Killer's warriors attacked Louis Hamilton's command and very nearly caught and killed Isaac Coates. In July, Pawnee Killer's men killed Lieutenant Kidder and his party on Beaver Creek. For years, this implacable marauder ranged the southern plains, raiding settlements, engaging the army, and killing travelers on the main overland roads. Though he attended the council between Indian leaders and the peace commissioners preceding the Medicine Lodge Treaty, less than a year later his warriors joined with the Cheyennes and Arapahos to attack Major George Forsythe at Beecher Island. After the Battle of Summit Springs, Pawnee Killer no longer had sufficient forces to be much of a threat. In 1870, he joined other Sioux leaders in discussions with agency officials about an impending visit of Sioux chiefs to Washington.

2. The three Dog Soldier chiefs, Bull Bear, Tall Bull, and White Horse, led their soldier band from the last free years of the 1850s, through the war-filled 1860s, and, except for Tall Bull, who was killed at Summit Springs, into the 1870s, the years of disintegration. As early as 1863, Bull Bear had agreed to attend a council with the whites, but the Cheyennes refused to let him go. In 1864 he joined with Black Kettle and other chiefs in the conference with Governor Evans that was followed by the Sand Creek massacre. Bull Bear was one of the chiefs who met with Hancock in April 1867. In November 1869, Bull Bear's Dog Soldiers moved into Cheyenne villages on reservation land near Camp Supply in Oklahoma, but apparently went to the Platte River country in the summer of 1870. In 1871, Bull Bear was in western Kansas with the Sioux. Back in Indian Territory in 1874, the Dog Soldiers joined other Cheyennes in the Red River War and, thereafter, settled into uneasy life on the reservation.

3. In 480 B.C., the Persian king Xerxes set out to invade Greece. The route of his huge army lay through the narrow pass of Thermopylae, where Leonidas, king of Sparta, and 8,000 men held out for three days until they were overrun and killed by the Persians.

4. Roman Nose was not a Dog Soldier and was never a tribal chief, but he was famous among the Plains Indians as the great war leader of the Southern Cheyennes. In 1865 the indomitable, ferocious Roman Nose organized and led the charge against the troops of General Connor's Powder River expedition and against Lieutenant Caspar Collins at Platte Bridge. In 1866, he visited Fort Wallace and warned the whites to abandon the Smoky Hill road. Isaac Coates, with the other observers on the Hancock expedition, thought Roman Nose the most conspicuous and impressive of all Indian leaders, not only because of his physical height and proud bearing but also because he was so obviously fearless and unin-

timidated by Hancock's large military force. In August 1867, warriors under the command of Roman Nose and other leaders attacked Captain George Armes near Fort Hays, killing three troopers and wounding thirty five. Although Tall Bull, Bull Bear, and White Horse signed the Medicine Lodge Treaty, Roman Nose refused and remained separate from the other leaders.

Just before the Beecher Island fight of 1868, Roman Nose unwittingly ate food that broke his protective medicine. When he learned of his mistake, he realized he would have to go through a purification ceremony to regain the power of the medicine but was unwilling to take the time to do so after Major George Forsythe's scouts were discovered on Beecher Island. As he rode at the head of the charge, Roman Nose was sure that he would be killed. Indeed, he was shot through the back and fell off his horse. He died later that evening.

Chapter Five

1. Elizabeth Akers Allen (1832–1911), "Rock Me to Sleep," 1860.
2. George A. Custer, *My Life on the Plains*, 56, 57, 58.
3. Ibid., 60, 61.
4. Ibid., 63.

Chapter Six

1. Roman Emperor Vespasian (A.D. 9–A.D. 79) built the Colosseum in Rome. His son, Titus Flavius Domitianus (A.D. 51–A.D. 96), carried on all sorts of bloody games in his father's amphitheater. In Greek mythology, Hecate was the goddess of graveyards, among many other responsibilities.

2. Petroleum V. Nasby, pen name of journalist and satirist David Ross Locke (1838–1888).

3. King Philip, who died in 1676, was chief of the Wampanoag Indians of the East Coast. He led the New England tribes in a general war against the whites that resulted in the permanent destruction of the Indian culture. Powhatan (who died in 1618) was chief of the Powhatan tribe in Virginia. His daughter was Pocahontas.

4. The Delawares, of Algonquian origin, originally lived in the area that now comprises Delaware, New Jersey, and eastern Pennsylvania. As white men appropriated their lands, they were driven westward, finally ending up in parts of eastern Kansas and Oklahoma. Skillful scouts and hunters, they were hired as guides by the army. As early as 1857, a Delaware chief named Fall Leaf was guiding military expeditions in western Kansas. Hancock's guide may have been the same person.

5. Edward Payson Weston (1839–1929) was a famous American walker who accomplished some amazing feats of speed and distance. In 1861, he walked from Boston to Washington, a distance of 443 miles, in 208 hours in order to attend Lincoln's inauguration. In 1909, at the age of seventy, Weston walked from New York to San Francisco in 104 days.

Chapter Seven

1. James B. "Wild Bill" Hickok (1837–1876) has been celebrated in print and film as the prototypical frontiersman-gunfighter. Among the most famous of all the colorful characters who populated the plains in the 1860s and 1870s, Hickok served as scout with the cavalry for only a few years before moving on to be a U.S. Marshall and an actor in Buffalo Bill Cody's Wild West Show. He was admired by Custer and Stanley, among many others, for his courage and knowledge of the country. During the Civil War, he had been a highly valued scout for federal commanders in southwest Missouri and Indian Territory. Despite a flair for the garish, he was a genuine article and was well liked and respected by the men of the Seventh Cavalry. Wild Bill was killed in a Deadwood saloon when he carelessly sat with his back to an open door. He was holding two pair—aces and eights—the "dead man's hand."

2. William Averill "Medicine Bill" Comstock was born in Michigan in 1842. By the time he was eighteen, he was an experienced frontiersman and Indian trader in the Platte River country. In January 1867, General Custer wrote to Captain Keogh at Fort Wallace asking that Comstock, who had been serving as a scout there since 1865, be sent to Fort Riley for duty with the Seventh Cavalry. Medicine Bill was back at Fort Wallace by the middle of February. In the third week of April, Custer then requested that Comstock be sent to Fort Hays to guide his expedition to the Platte and south to the Republican River.

Custer thought that Comstock, who was known as the best of the scouts of the southern plains, had both the knowledge of Indians and familiarity with the country to make him the ideal guide for the trip. He also found Medicine Bill a valuable and stimulating companion. From the very beginning of the march, the expedition depended on Comstock's skill and instincts for its survival. On July 13, he brought Custer's command to Fort Wallace, intact but exhausted and reduced in size. Despite years of living with the Cheyennes and gaining their friendship, Comstock's luck ran out in 1868 when he and a companion, Abner Grover, were ambushed by a group of young Cheyenne braves. Comstock was killed and Grover severely wounded.

3. Robert G. Athearn, *William Tecumseh Sherman and the Settlement of the West*, 152.

4. Document #240, 65.

5. Ibid., 66.

Chapter Eight

1. Kicking Bird was a Kiowa tribal chief. He was one of the Kiowas who had warned the army early in 1867 that war would come as soon as the grass was up. With Satanta and other chiefs of the Kiowas, Comanches, Arapahos, and Cheyennes, he signed the Medicine Lodge Treaty. His speech to Hancock was an honest statement of his conviction that peace with the whites was the only way for the Kiowas. He did his best to lead his people toward accommodation with the whites until his death in 1875.

2. For many years a principal chief of the Arapahos, Little Raven was a leader in forging peaceful relations, first between the tribes and then between the Arapahos and the whites. In 1840, he had called together chiefs of the Comanches, Cheyennes, Kiowas, Arapahos, and Kiowa-Apaches to arrange for a cease-fire among the tribes. By 1859, Little Raven was well known and respected as a friend by settlers in Colorado. In 1863, he took his people to Fort Lyon to receive their annuity goods, where the Arapahos were described by army officers as "destitute." In the general war that followed the Sand Creek massacre, Little Raven was one of the few chiefs who kept his people out of the fighting. In October 1865, Little Raven joined with other Arapaho and Cheyenne chiefs in signing a truce with the government. In August 1869, he intervened between the Cheyennes and the government, successfully negotiating for a reservation agreement more satisfactory to the Indians. By 1870, Little Raven and his Arapahos had more or less settled down to reservation life in Oklahoma Territory.

3. In October 1865, a peace commission met with the Arapahos, Kiowas, Comanches, Cheyennes, and Apaches on the Little Arkansas River, where they signed a treaty setting aside land for the tribes south of the Arkansas River.

4. Document #240, 105.

5. Famous throughout the southern plains for his fierce, unyielding determination to drive the white man out of his country, Satanta was also a great orator. Isaac Coates was so impressed with his eloquence and dignity that he did not want to believe the story about Satanta flipping the tails of his major general's coat when he was stealing horses at Fort Dodge, but there are so many tales about Satanta's incorrigible behavior that the story is probably true. Donald Worcester,

a contributor to *American Indian Leaders*, says that in one battle Satanta confused army troops by sounding bugle calls on his own bugle.

Satanta was born in 1820 and soon became recognized as a war leader. As the whites continued to slaughter the buffalo and drive the Indians out of white-occupied territory, the Kiowas split into two factions: One was led by Kicking Bird and other chiefs who favored peace, the other, by Satanta and Satank, who were determined to carry on the fight as long as they could. Satanta was one of the principal Indian leaders at the Medicine Lodge Creek councils, and he signed the treaty.

After the Battle of the Washita, Satanta narrowly escaped being hanged by Sheridan. In 1870, Satanta defiantly led a raid into Texas. He and Satank were arrested and ordered to stand trial for murder. Satank committed suicide by attacking a guard and waiting to be shot by the other guards. Satanta was set free in 1873, but a year later he was thought to have been involved in another raid and was sent to prison. In 1878, an old man without hope, he jumped to his death from a prison window.

6. Jesse H. Leavenworth (1807–1885) was an Indian agent for the Kiowas and Comanches. Although he accompanied Wynkoop on the Hancock expedition, Isaac Coates does not mention him. Leavenworth was unpopular with Indians and controversial in the Indian Bureau. He was frequently accused of corruption but was never tried or convicted on the charge.

Chapter Nine

1. Henry M. Stanley, *My Early Travels and Adventures in America*, 87.
2. Robert M. Utley, *Cavalier in Buckskin: George Armstrong Custer and the Western Military Frontier*, 50.

Chapter Ten

1. George A. Custer, *My Life on the Plains*, 115, 116.
2. Ibid., 127.
3. Ibid., 130, 131.
4. Ibid., 146, 147, 148, 149.
5. Robert M. Utley, *Life in Custer's Cavalry: Diaries and Letters of Albert and Jennie Barnitz, 1867–1868*, 69, 70, 71, 72, 73.
6. George A. Custer, *My Life on the Plains*, 173.

7. Lieutenant Lyman S. Kidder was a promising young officer but had little experience fighting Indians. He was assigned to the Second U.S. Cavalry at Fort Sedgwick, where he and his small detachment of very young men were ordered to carry dispatches from General Sherman to General Custer through country infested with hostile Indians. His body was later exhumed by his father and reinterred in a cemetery in St. Paul, Minnesota.

8. Robert M. Utley, *Life in Custer's Cavalry: Diaries and Letters of Albert and Jennie Barnitz, 1867–1868*, 270.

Chapter Eleven

1. Transcript of the 1867 court-martial of George Armstrong Custer, National Archives, Records of the Office of the Judge Advocate General, Record Group 153.

Chapter Twelve

1. Fort McRae was established in 1863, ten miles east of the present-day town of Truth or Consequences, New Mexico, to guard travelers on El Camino Real. It was abandoned in 1876.

2. Surgeon General Joseph K. Barnes (1817–1883) had entered the army in 1840. He assumed the duties of surgeon general in 1864 and held the post until 1882, when he retired.

Chapter Thirteen

1. Rachel Sherman Thorndike, *The Sherman Letters*, 321.

2. Robert G. Athearn, *William Tecumseh Sherman and the Settlement of the West*, 223.

3. George Bird Grinnell, *The Fighting Cheyennes*, 309.

Bibliography

Ashburn, P.M. *A History of the Medical Department of the United States Army.* Boston, 1929.

Athearn, Robert G. *William Tecumseh Sherman and the Settlement of the West.* Norman, Okla., 1956.

Berthrong, Donald J. *The Southern Cheyennes.* Norman, Okla., 1963.

Catton, Bruce. *Glory Road.* Garden City, N.Y., 1954.

Clary, David A. "The Role of the Army Surgeon in the West: Daniel Weisel at Fort Davis, Texas, 1868–1872." *Western Historical Quarterly* 3 (1972).

Coates, Truman. *A Genealogy of Moses and Susanna Coates.* Privately printed. Oxford, Pa., 1906.

Custer, Elizabeth. *Tenting on the Plains.* Norman, Okla., 1971.

Custer, George A. *My Life on the Plains.* Edited by Milo Milton Quaife. Lincoln, Nebr., 1966.

Davis, Theodore R. "A Summer on the Plains." *Harper's New Monthly Magazine* 36 (February 1868).

Edmunds, R. David (ed.) *American Indian Leaders.* Lincoln, Nebr., 1980.

Frost, Lawrence A. *The Court-Martial of General George Armstrong Custer.* Norman, Okla., 1968.

Grant, Ulysses S. *Personal Memoirs of U. S. Grant.* 2 vols. New York, 1885.

Grinnell, George B. *The Fighting Cheyennes.* Norman, Okla., 1956.

Hafen, LeRoy R. *The Overland Mail, 1849–1869.* Cleveland, Ohio, 1926.

Holbrook, Stewart H. *The Story of American Railroads.* New York, 1948.

Hyde, George E. *Spotted Tail's Folk: A History of the Brulé Sioux.* Norman, Okla., 1961.

Johnson, Randy, and Nancy P. Allan. *Find Custer! The Kidder Tragedy.* Lockport, Ill., 1990.

Lee, Wayne C., and Howard C. Raynesford. *Trails of the Smoky Hill.* Caldwell, Idaho, 1980.

Lewellyn, Karl N., and E. Adamson Hoebel. *The Cheyenne Way.* Norman, Okla., 1941.

Stanley, Henry M. *My Early Travels and Adventures in America.* Lincoln, Nebr., 1982.

Underhill, Ruth M. *Red Man's America.* Chicago, 1955.

U.S. Congress. "Difficulties with the Indian Tribes." 41 Cong., 2 sess., House Executive Document No. 240 (Serial 1425).

Utley, Robert M. *Cavalier in Buckskin: George Armstrong Custer and the Western Military Frontier.* Norman, Okla., 1988.

————. *Frontier Regulars: The United States Army and the Indian, 1866–1891.* New York, 1973.

————. *Life in Custer's Cavalry: Diaries and Letters of Albert and Jennie Barnitz, 1867–1868.* Lincoln, Nebr., 1977.

Wynkoop, Edward W. *The Tall Chief: The Autobiography of Edward W. Wynkoop.* Edited by Christopher B. Berboth. Denver, 1993.

Index

About the Author

W.J.D. KENNEDY retired as executive director of ACCORD Associates, a nonprofit conflict management organization. He has written numerous articles about conflict management for professional journals and is co-author (with Susan Carpenter) of *Managing Public Disputes*.

Mr. Kennedy received a Bachelor's Degree in English Literature from Harvard College, and later was a member of the 10th Mountain Division during World War II. While living in St. Paul, Minnesota, he served on the Minnesota Human Rights Commission and as chairman of a Governor's Indian Action Committee.

Mr. Kennedy lives in Boulder, Colorado, with his wife, Lucretia, who is Isaac Coates's great granddaughter. *On the Plains with Custer and Hancock* is the result of five years of research.